A View from the Cockpit

WINNING THE AMERICA'S CUP

A View from the Cockpit

WINNING THE AMERICA'S CUP

by Robert N. Bavier, Jr.

Illustrated with photographs

MORRIS ROSENFELD & SONS

JOHN HOPF

GEORGE SILK

New York DODD, MEAD & COMPANY

Also by Robert N. Bavier, Jr.

SAILING TO WIN

THE NEW YACHT RACING RULES

FASTER SAILING

Library of Congress Catalog Card Number: 66-23218

Printed in the United States of America

Designed by Sidney Feinberg

Dedication

It is normal to dedicate a book to a single person, but an America's Cup campaign is such a team effort as to make this inappropriate. Therefore, this book has a multiple dedication.

It is dedicated first of all to the forgotten men of the team, without whom there would have been no *Constellation*. I refer, of course, to the syndicate members who paid our monumental bills, who shared our anguish when we were losing, but who were given no public credit in our victory. It is high time their identity be unveiled! The men who made *Constellation* possible are:

JOHN ANDERSON II
JOHN ASTOR
GEORGE F. BAKER, JR.
C. HASCALL BLISS
GEORGE T. BOWDOIN
CUMMINS CATHERWOOD
BRIGGS S. CUNNINGHAM
JOHN T. DORRANCE, JR.
D. C. ELWOOD
ROGER S. FIRESTONE
AVARD E. FULLER
WALTER S. GUBELMANN
STANLEY C. HOPE
GEORGE F. JOHNSON
FRANCIS L. KELLOGG
DAVID O'D. KENNEDY
GEORGE M. MOFFETT, JR.
EDMOND C. MONELL
JAMES J. O'NEILL

CHARLES S. PAYSON
THOR RAMSING
ERIC RIDDER
JOSEPH E. RIDDER
WILLIAM RUDKIN
RUDOLPH J. SCHAEFER
JUDSON B. SHAFER
CHAUNCEY STILLMAN
DUDLEY F. UNDERHILL
ARCHBOLD VAN BEUREN
HAROLD S. VANDERBILT
GILBERT VERNEY
FRANCIS D. WETHERILL

It is dedicated also to the best 12-Meter crew ever assembled, a crew whose competence was matched only by its good humor.

It is dedicated to Eric Ridder for giving me the chance to steer his dream—the finest racing sailboat in the world.

And finally, the most important of all, it is dedicated to my wife, Charlotte, for encouraging me to accept this challenge and for never letting me lose confidence through the long pressure-packed summer.

Acknowledgments

The drama and excitement of racing for the America's Cup cannot be captured with words alone. Without fine photos this book would be but half a book and hence I am so indebted to the photographers, Morris Rosenfeld & Sons, John Hopf and George Silk, who have made it a whole one. The bulk of the photos were from Morris Rosenfeld & Sons, and I am particularly indebted to Stan Rosenfeld for the hours he spent with me going through some 5000 prints to select the 87 we used.

I am indebted also to Marge Keller for typing the manuscript from my almost undecipherable scribble.

I want to call attention to the fact that the chapter entitled "Breaking *Eagle*'s Heart" first appeared in slightly different form in *Sports Illustrated*, August 16, 1965, under the title "The Race That Beat the Bird."

In particular, I am appreciative of the warm, generous and moving Foreword by my good friend, Peter Scott. In this Foreword Peter is all too willing to shoulder a share of responsibility for *Sovereign*'s defeat, but I hope the book makes it clear that it was largely a question of his having a slower "horse."

Foreword

To me the words "America's Cup" mean the most publicised and spectacular failure of my life. To Bob Bavier they mean the exact opposite.

Down the years those two words have meant quite different things to different people: to Sir Thomas Lipton a life-long dream which obstinately refused to come true; to the Earl of Dunraven a long tale of acrimony and international dispute; to Sir Tom Sopwith an agonising near-miss that could not be recouped; to Harold Vanderbilt a glittering record of successful defence.

The America's Cup is unique as the only top prize of a sport which has never changed hands in more than a century, and still retains front page news value. As one of the world's few still-unconquered Everests it continues to capture the imagination of millions, in spite of the ignominious defeats so often meted out by its defenders.

Constellation's supremacy over *Sovereign* was one of the most convincing in the Cup's history. The yacht's names in this context include not only the hulls, the spars, the sails, the instruments, but also the helmsmen and the crews, and there will long be argument on which of these factors were primarily responsible for the result.

A part of the answer will be found in this book, and only one aspect of the story does not seem to me to emerge clearly enough, which may not be so surprising, because the author is a modest man. The point should not be missed that *Constellation* was sailed with superlative skill by a great natural 12-Metre helmsman—probably the best in the world.

Bob Bavier is that rare combination—a brilliant helmsman who can write. The sub-title of his book discloses the final outcome, should the reader not know it already, yet Bob manages to maintain the excitement and suspense all through the book, and even into the anti-climactic climax. The result cast a rosy glow over all that went before in *Constel-*

lation's hectic summer of preparation.

It is sometimes difficult to prevent that same result from giving a bitter taste to the whole of *Sovereign's* equally hectic summer. And yet until the last four races of the season, things had gone well enough for *Sovereign.* Off Portsmouth, England, and Newport, Rhode Island, *Sovereign* had battled with her near-sister ship *Kurrewa V* for the honour of challenging and had won by the narrowest of margins after a summer of wonderfully exciting racing. Whatever happened we should now at least be second in the America's Cup!

That the chances of winning were not good was first borne in upon us when *Sovereign* was too often beaten in early practice races by *Sceptre,* the badly defeated 12-metre of the previous challenge. Further writing appeared on the wall when we first saw the American 12-metres at Newport and were able to compare their hulls and their masts and their sails with our own. Their refinement at once appeared much greater than ours, but at that stage there was nothing we could do about it, and there was still a tiny hope that our assessments were wrong, that the indications of major hull improvement derived from the tank tests on the hull model were right, and that Olin Stephens's *Constellation* was not the startling advance on all previous 12-metres that her battles with *American Eagle* suggested.

"By 12:15 on 15th September, 1964," we used to say, "we shall know the answer, for by that time we shall have been going to windward in close company with *Constellation* for a quarter of an hour." And when that time came, our worst fears were confirmed. We could not sail as close to the wind as *Constellation* by several degrees—perhaps as much as 5°. The rougher the sea, the greater the discrepancy.

Having discovered that what we believed to be the best compromise between angle on the wind and speed through the water was simply not good enough, it seemed only right to try something different. We tried sailing fast and free, and we tried pinching up and accepting a slower speed. These experiments of desperation only put us further astern, but they had to be tried.

With the wind behind her *Sovereign* was no slower than *Constellation,* though bad judgement, especially in the selection of the right-sized spinnaker, lost us time on most of the runs—as much as 7 minutes on one of them. For some sad reason we could not break loose from a belief that a huge parachute which had pulled us splendidly in calm water could be made to do the same in the steep and confused seas caused by the spectator fleet. But it was the effect of these seas on *Sovereign*'s windward performance which seemed to be the prime cause of our downfall. We seemed to hobby-horse much more than *Constellation*, and each time we pitched forward the boat seemed to stop in her tracks. How much this had to do with the shape of her hull, or with the mast, or the sails, or with the helmsman's inability to sidle her through the seas will never be known. One thing is certain: it had nothing whatsoever to do with her crew; and I am convinced that apart from steering and decision-making the crew of *Sovereign* was every bit as skilful and competent as the crew Bob describes so vividly in this book. They were a splendid team all through the summer and never more so than in the last dark days of defeat.

So we were beaten—badly beaten—a combination which failed miserably to compete with a superior combination, but after all we had done our best. The series had been conducted without a single unhappy incident or protest. Much had been learnt about 12-metres, their design, their sails, their handling. New friendships had been made and old ones confirmed. Even as we sailed back into Newport Harbour after the last race of the Cup series I knew that for me the effort had been worth while. Tony Boyden, *Sovereign*'s owner, has told me that he felt the same, even on that last bitter evening.

I was delighted when Bob Bavier invited me to write this Foreword to his book, for we have been friends for many long years, serving together in the International Yacht Racing Union. It has given me an opportunity to give a very brief impression of my own feelings about those parts of his story with which I was personally involved.

It has also given me an opportunity to pay tribute to the brilliant performance of *Constellation* and to all who had a part in it, particularly my opposite number, and good friend, her helmsman.

PETER SCOTT

Slimbridge, Gloucestershire, England
May, 1966

Contents

A View from the Cockpit

WINNING THE AMERICA'S CUP

"Constellation," looking her loveliest and going her fastest on July 24. Minutes later she lost her mast—the darkest day of the summer. Two days later she beat "American Eagle" for the first time and thereafter went on to glory.

Early Days

As DICK GOENNEL AND I bounced our way from Oyster Bay across Long Island Sound to Noroton Harbor, if anyone but sea gulls had been watching they would surely have thought we were out of our minds. Maybe even the gulls did—and maybe they were right. It was a Saturday in early April 1964, the sun had just set and a 20-knot nor'wester was throwing frigid spray into our faces as our Boston Whaler bucked homeward. We were making 20 knots in hopes of reaching our mooring before darkness added to our numbing discomfort.

Early that morning we had skimmed across the Sound in the reverse direction, flushing huge flocks of Broadbill, which saw no reason yet to wing north to colder climes. In between we had spent hours sailing a 68-foot dark-hulled sloop whose numbers $\frac{12}{\text{US }14}$ proclaimed her to be the fourteenth 12-Meter built in the United States. All day long we had shifted mains, changed jibs, adjusted leads, set spinnaker, doused it, set another, jibed it, ripped it, set another and another and another, repeated each maneuver ad infinitum (even the ripping, from time to time). And as we bounded homeward, Dick and I knew that early next morning we would be heading back to Oyster Bay for.more, much more, of the same. For our boat was *Nereus*, trial horse for the new 12-Meter *Constellation*, then building as a candidate for defense of the America's Cup. And we were part of *Constellation*'s crew.

Those who aspire to defend America's Cup will accept this as sufficient explanation for our willingness, even joy, in such self-torture. And all racing yachtsmen will appreciate the need for a dedicated effort of body and mind to get the most out of the superb racing machines which compete for this most revered of sailing trophies. Those who fall in neither category might wonder why we were out sailing in April in preparation for a September race which we might not even be selected for. This book will attempt to give the answers and to portray the tensions, emotions, disappointments and exhilarations of campaigning for the America's Cup.

The Invitation

For me it all began with a phone call in October 1963 from Eric Ridder, who proposed we have lunch to discuss something he hoped would interest me. We had barely got seated at the New York Yacht Club when Eric announced he was part of the syndicate headed by Walter Gubelmann to build an America's Cup candidate and was to be her skipper. He then asked if I would like to sign on as alternate helmsman and tactician? In the next breath (and before I had caught mine) he avowed that if at any time he felt incapable of getting best results from the new boat, he would let someone else try.

It was reassuring to learn that Eric realized how frustrating it would be to spend a summer on a boat which was not being sailed up to her potential.

His credentials, however, were impressive—winner of an Olympic Gold Medal in Six Meters, years of successful distance racing on the 73-foot yawl *Windigo*. He had already signed on Larry Scheu, member of *Vim's* stirring effort in 1958, Buddy Bombard, also a *Vim* alumnus and veteran of the winning America's Cup efforts on *Weatherly* in 1962, and Fred Kulicke, a young stalwart on *Windigo*.

As we talked over coffee, it seemed we were off to a good start. We? Two hours ago I knew nothing of the invitation and here I was already thinking in terms of devoting six months to the most concentrated sailing effort of a lifetime—three months of weekends spent away from my family—three more months of sailing every day, all day. There was, I knew, no other way to approach the quest for the role of defending the America's Cup, and I would be unhappy with any other way. But how would Charlotte feel, how would my boss, how well could I afford the extra expense of such an effort?

I told Eric I would let him know in ten days. That very afternoon I got enthusiastic approval from Bob Rimington, my boss at *Yachting*. Bob understood this was a once-in-a-lifetime opportunity. A three-month safari to Africa would have been one thing, but three months in quest of the America's Cup was O.K. by *Yachting*.

"Constellation's" great crew (left to right, front row) Fenny Johnson, Dun Gifford, Buddy Bombard, (second row) Fred Kulicke, John Handel, Put Brown, Eric Ridder, Bob Bavier, (third row) Dick Enersen, Bob Connell, Steve Van Dyck, Larry Scheu, Rod Stephens and Dick Goennel.

That evening Charlotte and I talked it out over cocktails and on into the night, with me professing concern over being away so much and she urging that I accept. At first this was hard for me to understand, because Charlotte never acted overjoyed when I took off for a week to go ocean racing, and here she was urging that I get involved in something twenty times as long. She knew, however, that racing for the America's Cup was something special, and hence made light of the obstacles. Besides, she knew me better than I knew myself, and realized at once that I would accept eventually. She asked only that we rent a house in Newport in the summer so the whole family could share the experience, the excitement. Without a second thought about Newport prices, I said "Of course."

I could have called Eric the very next day, but instead I waited a full week, kidding myself (but fooling no one else) that there really was an element of doubt and that my pious announcements of concern over what Charlotte and the kids would do could possibly mean that I would not accept. The week which passed before I called Eric with my acceptance was valuable only because it allowed the enormity of the effort required to sink in.

Selecting the Crew

We now had only a bare nucleus of a crew, but had each section of the boat covered. Buddy Bombard was to be in charge of the foredeck. Buddy was short, built like a featherweight wrestler and as quick and active as one. He had a ready smile and a host of friends. It was impossible to walk a block down any street in Newport, Oyster Bay, Bermuda or anywhere else sailors gather without Buddy meeting someone (often a pretty girl) he knew well.

Larry Scheu, who was giving up his job to be able to sail, was to be deck boss amidships, with Freddy Kulicke already supplying muscle power. With Eric and me, the cockpit was already pretty well covered. We now had five out of an eleven-man crew and figured we would need two or three alternates to bring the total up to thirteen or fourteen.

Eric and I both felt that we wanted to concentrate on getting sailors of long and varied experience rather than just a bunch of strong backs with limited experience. And we wanted a compatible group above all

The beauty of functional design, on the eve of launching in Minneford's building shed.

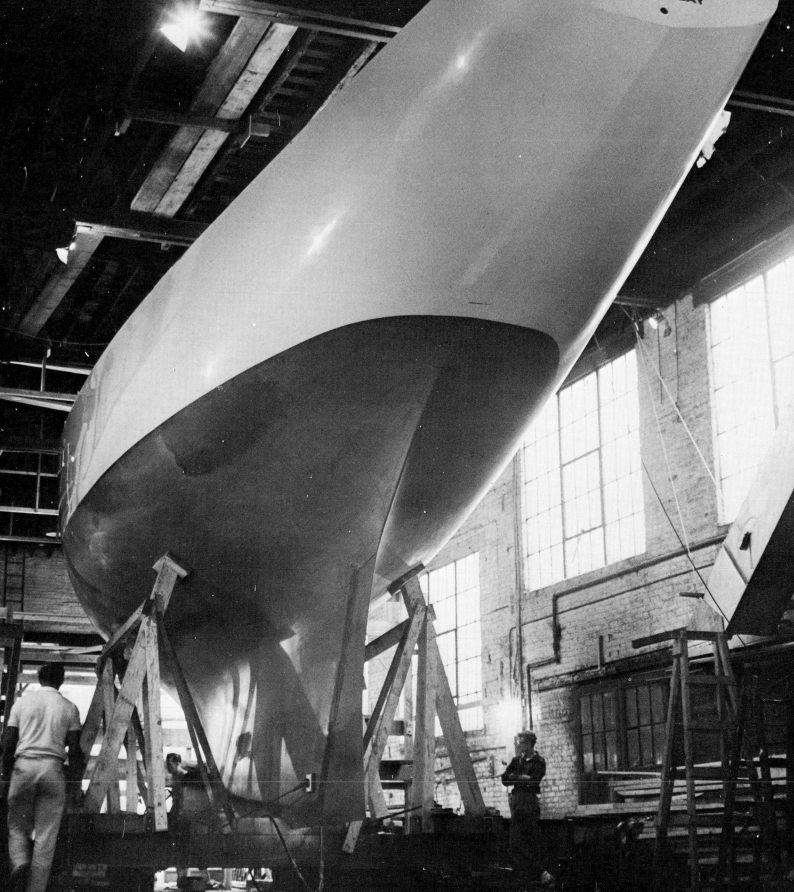

else. Twelve-Meter experience would be desirable, but only if we felt the candidate was a better sailor than someone without experience on Twelves. I, for example, had never set foot on one but hoped that a background of keen racing in everything from dinghies to ocean racers would, with a couple of months' experience on *Nereus*, make me at home when *Constellation* came along.

It was easy to find eager applicants. Eric, Buddy, Larry and I all knew lots of sailors, and all threw their names into the hopper for consideration. Friends suggested still others, and then there were a number of applicants who wrote telling of their availability. Eric and I met all of them, checked their records and finally came up with a selection of eleven regulars and three alternates. At the end of the summer ten of the regular crew were still on board and the eleventh, who was excellent, was benched only in favor of Rod Stephens at the beginning of the final trials when we felt a bit more experience in the cockpit was called for. All original fourteen were still with us when we sailed that last race against *Sovereign*. If a better crew has ever been assembled, I've never seen it.

As Twelves go, it was an old crew. Assisting thirty-year-old Buddy Bombard on the foredeck were forty-seven-year-old Dick Goennel and thirty-seven-year-old Fenny Johnson. Dick looked and acted ten years younger than he was, but was not selected for his quick coordination and strength, but rather because of his years of crewing as foredeck man for Corny Shields and other greats in Internationals, and for his many years of ocean racing to Bermuda (10 races), across the ocean, (both Atlantic and Pacific), and almost everywhere on keen boats. He had even sailed for three and a half years on a square rigger. His seamanship was as well known as his competitive drive. Above all, he never got the least bit ruffled in the tightest situations.

George Fennimore Johnson, better known as "Fenny," was chosen not because he was a syndicate member but because he was strong, quick and experienced in sail handling and so dedicated to an America's Cup effort that he was willing, even eager, to forsake his own brand-new 67-foot sloop *Challenge* to work his heart out before the mast on a Twelve. No one worked harder in practice or a race, and a measure of the man is the fact that after sailing together for nearly three months, half of the crew still didn't know Fenny was a syndicate member. By then he had been accepted on his merits as a hard-working, efficient

She seemed to be straining toward the sea, eager to prove her speed. "Constellation" was heavy but oh so graceful, huge yet with little wetted surface to cause drag.

and strong member of the crew. At starts his was the most exhausting job on board because it was he who trimmed the main by hand, prior to winching, during the customary circling maneuvers.

We have already introduced Larry Scheu and Fred Kulicke, who were signed on before me, but a few more words about their duties. Larry, because of his prior 12-Meter experience, his ability and also because he was older than the rest of the midship contingent, was put in charge of organizing this section of the boat. His personal activity was to trim the main sheet on the Barient 28 winch, a backbreaking job and one which also required judgment, since he was responsible for getting the proper trim prior to minor adjustments which might be called for from the cockpit. He also was first man to pull in the spinnaker sheet on a douse and in a tacking duel could take a turn on the linked coffee grinders. Larry attacked his trimming assignments with ferocity, mixed with good sense. I can still see his fierce grimace as he flailed at the spinnaker during a take-down. When Larry attacked a spinnaker, the poor sail just seemed to give up and came in meekly.

Fred's job was to handle all halyard winches and team on one of the coffee grinders while tacking. He also handled the coffee grinder controlling the spinnaker guy. His work on halyards was more involved than on most boats. It was necessary not only to winch them up fast but also to get exactly the right tension on our stretchy luff jibs for the weight of wind at the moment. At first this was done by marking the halyards and matching these marks to corresponding marks on the deck or below. Eventually, however, we came to a torque wrench which was faster and just as positive, provided Fred got it set to give the desired tension. By the time the important races rolled around, he always did. Fred started the summer as a somewhat brash youngster overly full of suggestions. He ended it as a man who could be counted on to do a job under fire.

The other three in the midships gang were all in their early twenties but had amassed as much sailing experience as many yachtsmen get in a lifetime. Bob Connell was a bull of a man, of medium height, stocky and hard as nails. Having finished college, he was an Ensign in the Navy, from which we rescued him for "international sporting competition." Bob had been on *Columbia* in 1962. He had crewed extensively on ocean racers and he was a top-flight skipper in the Lightning class. He concentrated on the coffee grinder winches not only while tacking but also for the spinnaker trim. When Bob wanted a sheet trimmed, it got trimmed. His station was adjacent to the cockpit, and while he seldom entered into our discussions, he always listened, and I could invariably tell which way he was thinking. By the end of the summer it was dawning on me that Bob's opinion was almost always right. There were no jobs aboard he could not have done well.

The two tailers on the genoa were Steve Van Dyck and Don Wakeman. Tailing those wire sheets, casting them off with tons of pressure on them, trimming hard and fast by hand during the tacks to minimize the amount of coffee grinder work was a job requiring strength and great quickness. They also controlled the jib trim, unless or until corrected by the helmsman. I seldom corrected either.

Steve was also always on the spinnaker sheet whenever it was set, and hence *Constellation* was almost literally in his hands downwind. He was of medium build but strong and quick. Above all else he concentrated on the job at hand and considered it a personal affront if the spinnaker broke. His background was serving on *Columbia* in 1962, the trans-Atlantic Race on *Dyna* in 1963, followed by the Fastnet, several Bermuda and other ocean races and several years of closed-course racing in Blue Jays, Lightnings and other small boats. His life was sailing, interrupted in the winter by attending Wilkes College.

Don Wakeman was a fugitive from the Army on the same basis in which we sprung Bob Connell from the Navy. His sailing background was largely in ocean racers. And some background!—trans-Atlantic, trans-Pacific and out to Australia, Sydney Hobart Race, Bermuda Races,

Fastnet Races and many lesser events. He had worked in boatyards, and was particularly adept at rigging and tuning. He seemed to spend half the day aloft on *Constellation*, and her superbly tuned rig was in large measure his doing. Don was the first man on board in the morning and the last to leave at night.

As navigator, we signed on K. Dun (Dunny) Gifford, a Harvard law student with a background of successful ocean and small-boat racing, particularly in the Flying Dutchman class. Dunny's experience as a navigator was a bit limited, but he avowed he could learn, and we wanted to add more brawn in the cockpit than Eric and I could supply. Dunny did indeed learn and did a faultless job of always knowing exactly where we were. His judgment in tactics and sail trim was also excellent. Perhaps his greatest contribution was his constant good humor, wit and perseverance, especially when things were going poorly. There was no more popular member of the crew.

The above gave us our regular eleven-man crew which we hoped would go through the campaign intact. But in case of illness, injury or ineptitude, every Twelve needs a bench, and for this purpose we signed on Put Brown, Dick Enersen and John Handel. Put was a junior at Williams, where he was a star on the swimming team. His sailing experience included both middle-distance and small-boat racing. Dick Enerson came from the West Coast, and despite being in his early twenties, his ocean-racing experience included both trans-Atlantic and trans-Pacific races. John Handel, a New York stockbroker, also had an extensive ocean-racing background. He contributed a steady flow of jokes which did much to ease tension during some of the darker days of the summer. The only racing any of them did all summer was on the New York Yacht Club Cruise, not because they were not good, but because our regulars turned out to be too good and too healthy. *Constellation*'s three alternates were, however, very much members of the team. They helped sail our trial horse, *Nereus*, helped keep *Constellation* and her gear in top shape, and helped keep the regulars on their toes. They could have stepped in to do a good job at almost any position on board, and despite certain disappointment at not sailing in a single trial race, they were all there, all still smiling bravely at the end of September when *Sovereign* went down to her fourth defeat.

In August we were to make a truly key addition to our crew—Rod Stephens—but more about him at the appropriate time.

Winter Work

Our crew was all picked by the end of January. Our plan was to start sailing *Nereus*, our trial horse, in early March. I thought that too early—and said so—because I feared the edge might come off our crew if we practiced for three months without an opponent. Eric still held out for March, but when outfitting was delayed, it turned out we couldn't sail before April anyway. Perhaps this was anticipated when March was set as a target, but in any event it turned out to my liking. In retrospect, two months of drill with no one to compete against seemed ample, if not excessive.

In the meantime each in his own way started getting into top shape. Most of the twenty-year-olds already were. Of the others, Dick Goennel worked out with weights, Fenny Johnson headed for a gym near his home, I started walking instead of riding to the train. Eric knocked off cocktails. There wasn't much more for most of us to do. Olin and Rod Stephens and many on their designing team were intensely busy, not on the basics of hull or rig, all of which were long since decided, but on the countless little details which added together can spell the difference between a good boat and a great one. For my part, never having set foot on a Twelve, I felt at a loss to offer suggestions, however minor.

One day in February, however, at least half of the crew assembled at Minneford's to discuss the deck layout, arrangements of winches, cleats and leads. *Constellation*'s deck plan was painted on a loft floor and a crude cockpit mockup had been assembled of plywood. There were dummy winches of assorted sizes. We had great sport making believe we were trimming the genoa and clowning around, and we also did some hard thinking as to the proper location of fittings. One novel feature was the placement of the coffee grinders just forward of the cockpit so the tailers could operate from the cockpit. The mockup indicated that it would be practical and such later proved to be the case. In fact it was a wonderful arrangement, made better by the virtue of the few inches of relocation dictated by the mockup.

Constellation's deck, even on the solid motionless loft floor, seemed a precariously narrow place for eleven men to work on without falling overboard. By summer's end it seemed like the most natural place to be, even without toe rails, but on that cold winter day it struck me as an impossible platform to sail on.

I remember sitting in the helmsman's seat, checking the clearance of the wheel, the view of the dummy compass, speedometers, apparent wind indicators. Their location was also modified slightly, largely to adjust to Eric's height. I said little, not expecting to be spending much time there. It was fun, though, even behind that crude dummy wheel, to dream a bit and hope to have a chance behind the real wheel later on.

Almost every week during the winter I drove the forty minutes from Darien to Minneford's on City Island to watch *Constellation* taking shape. Progress seemed agonizingly slow. At first just lines on the lofting floor, then piles of laminated frames, but nothing resembling a boat. The precision of the laminations was beautiful, but it seemed that all the various components would never get together. Then one week all the frames were suddenly erected, and from then on progress was rapid.

Most of our sails were ordered in February. We decided to put our greatest trust in Ted Hood, whose sails had been so successful in the 1962 America's Cup campaign. As an initial order we specified two 12-ounce mains (costing approximately $4000 each), one slightly fuller than the other; two 9-ounce genoas; one No. 2 genoa—also 9 ounces; two 5-ounce genoas; one 3-ounce and one 2.2-ounce genoas and a ¾-ounce drifter. We also ordered six spinnakers of various foot sizes. Half were 1.5 ounces, half ¾ ounce. All were full size on the hoist, but all somewhat below the maximum allowed in width. We were convinced the common mistake in past years had been to carry chutes which were too big.

In addition to Hood, we went to Wally Ross of Hard Sails. From him we ordered mostly experimental sails—a two-ply main made up of two layers of 5-ounce Dacron, two genoas which were also two-ply and one 1.5-ounce spinnaker. Poor Wally. Except for the spinnaker, we ordered not a single standard sail, and the chance of coming up with a successful experimental sail was a dim one. He would have liked, I am sure, just to have designed and built the best main or jib he could, without messing with any two-plys. Even though we knew the odds were against these sails, we felt we were covered by our basic Hood inventory and that our best chance for a breakthrough lay in ordering something truly different. The jibs were good, though not quite up to the Hoods, but the main, despite Wally's constant recutting, was a failure. Good two-ply mains may well evolve, but their stretch behavior is so different that more than a season is required to get the hang of them.

Afloat at Last

By late March, *Constellation* was beginning to look very much like a boat—a fast one—and our target of a May launching seemed assured.

Meanwhile, we had more immediate fish to fry. *Nereus* had been launched by Luders and towed across the Sound to Jakobson's Shipyard for outfitting. On April 7, all was in readiness.

It was a bright, cold day with a 10-knot northerly when Dick and I boarded the Whaler off Tom Ross' beach in Noroton for our first of many dashes across the Sound. Thirty minutes later we were at Jake's dock where *Nereus* was riding alongside her tender, *Chaperone*. Her tall spar told all the world that here was a Twelve. The stick itself was rugged enough, but the rigging seemed so light, so refined and simple, the spreaders looked, and were, so narrow. No ocean racer this, but truly a machine.

Half the crew was already there and within a half hour all but Bob Connell, who had not yet been sprung from the Navy, were on hand. We lugged the main on board—six of us. Its weight alone was enough to tell me that Twelves were a far cry from the small day racers and the 40-foot ocean racers I was used to.

I felt inadequate as the sails were being bent, lines reeved and all put in readiness for getting under way. As alternate helmsman I was, I assumed, sort of the executive officer, yet I felt too unfamiliar to give much direction. The 12-Meter veterans in our crew needed none, and I busied myself with keeping my eyes open and my mouth shut and tried to appear unconcerned, relaxed and more knowledgeable than I felt.

Inside an hour our tender, *Chaperone*, with Captain Bill Burton handling her in a deft fashion (which by summer's end we began to stop marveling at and accepted as standard procedure), had towed us clear and we made sail.

Once we had cast off under main and had set the genoa, all strangeness disappeared. Here was just another sailboat, larger than I was used to, but so responsive, so easily handled, so maneuverable that inside of minutes I began feeling a part of her. But neither on that day nor months later did I ever fail to marvel at the way a Twelve felt—a combination of power and drive, and at the same time a delicacy and refinement. The wind had lightened to little over 7 knots yet hard on the wind and reaching, the speedometers showed more than 8 knots. It was hard to believe they were accurate, but they were.

That first day we spent most of our time just getting the feel of *Nereus* and looking at the sails built for *Constellation.* In the cockpit I was finding out how incredibly close-winded a Twelve was. We seemed to be tacking to advantage in about 72°, fantastically close, I felt then, but nothing to what was to come later.

Over lunch we discussed crew assignments for various maneuvers, and after lunch set spinnaker. It went up smartly the very first time, but jibing caused some headaches. We were trying a new method Eric had developed for use on *Windigo.* Lines ran from each clew through the end of the pole, then inside the pole until they came out near the inboard end and ran through sheaves and then to cam jam cleats. When the spinnaker was set, the line to the tack was pulled taut and the tack snugged up to the end of the pole. The other line was eased well off and kept slack to let the clew run free. When jibing, the line to the tack was snapped out of its cam cleat, the pole was dipped and as it swung through the other line to the new tack, was hauled in quickly until the new tack was snugged up to the pole end. No one had to go forward of the mast and there were no connections or detachments to make. An ingenious rig, but we had trouble easing and trimming the jibing lines at the right moment, trouble getting the eased one to run free readily, trouble seating the other one promptly. In an ocean racer, when a jibe completed in one minute would be considered good and when one could hold her off for a moment to get the new tack line snugged up, the method could be excellent. But we had to be able to jibe in seconds, had to be able to jibe from a reach to a reach in a tight turn. The fact that we had trouble doing this that first day alarmed no one. We all felt it was just a matter of time before we could get it down pat.

In the weeks ahead, we tried different weights of jibing lines, both wire and Dacron and also Dacron-covered wire. We tried various different cam cleats. And we made some pretty snappy jibes. We also kept missing at times when the old tack line failed to run fast enough or when the cam jams were either hard to release or when they failed to hold. We also found it difficult at times to seat the tack home fast enough by hand in a breeze, requiring time-consuming winching in.

After a month of trying, and despite the fact that it often worked well, ten guys on board were ready to abandon the system. In fact we were fed up with it and alarmed at the trouble it could cause in a tight race. And we said so. Eric, however, retained confidence in the method. He felt it could be made to work eventually and hence we kept struggling with it.

All through April and well into May we were out in *Nereus,* sailing 8 hours each Saturday and Sunday. Sometimes it was light, sometimes 30 knots, sometimes warm and sunny, sometimes rainy and almost cold enough for sleet. But we never missed a day and despite our continued problems with the jibing method, we were getting sharp.

We experimented with setting spinnaker from a zipper sleeve, a modification of the Zipper Turtle developed by Ike Manchester. It worked well most of the time, but occasionally the sleeve got caught or fouled aloft. The advantage of the sleeve was to save the weight of zipper attached to the sail itself. We began to cool on the sleeve as time wore on but decided to stick with it through the June trials at least.

Despite these problems, we were developing confidence in ourselves. As for me, my early strangeness with Twelves, with their proper trim (which I called) and with the procedures for various maneuvers, had long since evaporated. *Nereus* seemed like a second home, and in my naïveté, she seemed so lively, so well balanced that I even thought she herself could make a pretty good contender with a modern rig and fine sails. I didn't then know how far Twelves had progressed, but would soon find out.

I was getting into shape, too, and found it almost fun to see if I could wind up the backstay before the winch grinders had flattened the genoa.

But I had one real regret. I had been signed on as alternate helmsman, but in a month and a half of sailing every weekend, I had the wheel little more often than when Eric had to go to the head—maybe two hours out of the one hundred we had sailed. Obviously Eric wanted every possible minute to get the feel of her, which was understandable. If I was to spell him at all, however, it seemed not unreasonable for me to be developing a feel, too. It was obvious, therefore, that Eric's plan was to keep the wheel at all times, a prospect which caused me some regret but one which I thought better not to complain about. The object was to win, and if we could best win by the skipper steering at all times, I had no cause to complain. There was, however, no law against feeling disappointment.

Tee Ridder and Barton Gubelmann (largely hidden) join forces in christening "Constellation."

Constellation Gets Launched

While we were putting *Nereus* through her paces, *Constellation* was coming along right on schedule. By late April it was safe to send out invitations for a May 16 launching. The hour was 4:00 P.M., which meant we had time to go to Oyster Bay, sail *Nereus* for 3 hours, dash home and still make the launching on time. There are no days off when campaigning for the America's Cup—not if you wish to win.

I hadn't seen *Constellation* for two weeks and wasn't prepared for the sight which greeted me upon arrival at Minneford. She was perfection in her gleaming paint job, her porcelainlike topsides. Her winches sparkled and her unique coffee grinders looked like some machines from another planet. Trim in the cockpit and below was in the finest yacht tradition, with superlative joiner work. It was lightweight, light as the rule allowed, but constructed with loving care.

Constellation looked big, looked powerful, and her tiny scimitar-

shaped rudder and wedge keel looked modern. She seemed almost to be moving as she stood poised on the elevator by the water's edge.

Guests were arriving in the hundreds, most of them yachtsmen I had known for years. A huge tent had been pitched to house the bar, the scores of tables and even a band yet! Most of us, however, spent more time out beside *Constellation*, keeping her company, keeping her (and ourselves) happy. Soon Eric and Walter Gubelmann, with their wives, Tee and Barton, mounted the speaker's and christening platform. It was a big platform, big enough for twenty-five syndicate members to join them and have their well-deserved day in the sun. Walter led off with a few appropriate remarks, most appropriate of which was his thanks to the syndicate (all of whom were mentioned by name and thanked for making the first stage of a dream possible). Eric followed with further remarks on how we aimed to do our best to complete the dream. Barton and Tee then grabbed a well-festooned champagne bottle and jointly took a mighty swing at *Constellation*'s bow chock, which somehow managed to stand the strain. Then as champagne sprayed skyward, Paul Coble pressed a button to lower the elevator. The ensuing voyage was the slowest *Constellation* ever traveled as she almost imperceptibly descended into her element. Eventually she

Soon after launching her 1000 pound Titanium-topped mast is stepped under designer Olin Stephens' (kneeling in business suit) watchful gaze.

floated free, trimmed perfectly and floating above her lines. Good—looks as if we can knock out that void in the keel and add ballast.

After the crowd cleared I went aboard, with Bill Cox, skipper of *American Eagle.* We were largely stripped below and had no secrets to hide. Our basic approach, too, was to be open about what we did have. Our theory was that if the opposition didn't have some of our good features, it probably would be too late for them to develop them. Besides, knowing that we had some interesting new developments might just make them nervous. Bill was as interested as I was, perhaps more so.

Next day we were back on *Nereus,* with our hearts not really in it. It was blowing hard and we had some trouble with the jibing method. Several of us got together afterward and tried again to persuade Eric to abandon it and go to the *Vim* method on *Constellation.* He listened but stuck to his guns. It wasn't the method but the details which were at fault, he said, and the latter could still be worked out. No one else thought so, but it was finally decided to work with it through the preliminary trials in June. At least our talk had the virtue of clearing the air. We now knew we were committed to the method for the next few weeks and had better make it work. If it didn't, we would get rid of it in time to perfect the other system before the more important trials.

Eagle Is Launched

Three days later we were all together again for another festive occasion—the launching of *American Eagle* at Luders Shipyard. More brave words—this time by Bill Luders, Pete duPont and Bill Cox. Bill Cox paid special tribute to his crew, citing each by name and avowing it was the best 12-Meter crew ever assembled. It was all beautifully and graciously stated, but we hoped he was wrong. We knew even then, though, that *Eagle* was the main obstacle between us and defense of the America's Cup.

She looked powerful but less graceful than *Constellation,* with greater flare, a broader stern and with noticeably more wetted surface. Her flat deck seemed the most clever feature. She, too, was beautifully built but not finished as superbly as *Constellation.* We felt we had won the beauty prize and hoped the adage "Handsome is as handsome does" would not apply to *American Eagle.*

Pete DuPont assists his granddaughter Wendy in christening "American Eagle" at Luders Shipyard.

As Charlotte and I drove home after the launching, she asked me what I thought. "I'll take *Constellation*," I replied and I meant it, not quite knowing why. "But Bill Cox will be tough," I added. Charlotte knew what I meant. I had raced against Bill in Lightnings, in International One Designs and in dinghies. I had beaten him too, many times, but more often Bill had beaten me. He was not just a fine sailor but one who lived, dreamed and planned sailing while not on the water. We both knew he would be going all out to beat us every minute, day and night, in the months ahead, knew it would take a superhuman effort to beat him. I felt we had a chance, a good chance, but wondered if Eric knew what a cool customer he was up against. Being objective, I had to rate Bill over Eric. But *Eagle* and her crew over *Constellation* and hers? That just might be another story.

We Sail *Constellation*

A few days later the big day arrived. Her spar stepped, winches and gear installed, we took *Constellation* out for her first sail. We were used to Twelves by now, but this was not just another sail, this was not *Nereus* but instead, we hoped, the greatest Twelve ever built. Would she measure up?

We were all smiles as we lugged sails on board. It was a beautiful spring day, with a gentle breeze from the west. *Nereus* went out first with Briggs Cunningham, the America's Cup winner in 1958 with

"Constellation's" scimitar shaped rudder, smaller than ever before seen on a Twelve. "Eagle's" (right), though small too, had more area and was more conservative.

Columbia, as skipper and with a crew of our alternates plus keen sailing veterans.

We hoisted main, cast off and started running toward Execution Light and the Sound. *Nereus* was a hot light-weather boat and had beaten *Columbia* six years before in just this sort of weather. We ran under main alone not more than 100 yards apart and we talked ourselves into expecting *Nereus,* with her larger main, to pull away. She didn't. We babbled with excitement, as if this crude test really was conclusive. At least it was encouraging, and I caught Olin Stephens with a slight grin on his face.

I was pretty sure Olin was grinning because he had designed *Constellation* to go in a breeze. She was big, heavy and with a minimum amount of sail, yet here she was running well in light air. Olin had managed to give *Constellation* very little wetted surface and hoped this would make her lively in light air. Hence this crude test against a boat recognized for her light air ability *was* something to grin about. We were to confirm the validity of this first indication later on.

Abeam of Execution, both boats set spinnaker—we waiting until *Nereus* had hers drawing before showing off with a snappy set. *Con-*

stellation slowly drew away. Huge grins and many wisecracks all around now. For 15 miles we ran together, and by the time we were off Oyster Bay, *Constellation* was a half mile ahead. By the talk you would think the America's Cup was ours already.

After lunch we set genoas and again held our breath while we beat back together. We needn't have held it. Briggs had *Nereus* in the groove, we were wandering a bit more, but *Constellation* ate out. She footed just a shade faster, but how she wanted to point! We would bear off, let *Nereus* get two lengths abeam of us and to weather, and inside of half a mile we would have a safe leeward. I persuaded Eric to let me try her. Same result. We were on air. The helm was a little harder than I would have liked, but Olin assured me she was designed to go best with 4° to 5° of angle on the rudder, and from that time on I never complained about the constant tug of weather helm. By summer's end I had grown to love it.

Late in the day the wind piped up to 18 knots. We heeled readily but then stopped with the lee deck well clear of the water, and now we really creamed *Nereus*. What a beginning!

In the ensuing two weeks our confidence mounted still further. We took *Nereus* with ease in all strengths of wind on all points of sailing.

One day we met *Columbia*, sailed with her for a while and left her behind.

Eagle was out too, looking sharp, but as if by mutual agreement we waved, then went our separate ways and never did hook up.

We still had occasional trouble with our jibing method. And some of our new gadgets were flops. For example, we had a "quick jib change device" under our forward deck. It consisted of a track onto which a second jib was attached with special hanks. On the forestay was a switch just above the deck. Upon changing, the switch was opened and the jib which was up was lowered swiftly, detaching itself automatically as it shot past the open switch. Next the halyard was attached to the alternate jib below decks, the switch closed and the new sail hoisted smartly up through the forward hatch. It sounded great, looked great, but the first time we tried it, it took nineteen *minutes* to make the change, instead of the nineteen seconds we rather hoped for. We eventually got it down to several minutes, but never fast enough, and hence out it came. The idea, I feel, is still sound. The trouble came because we couldn't get the hanks to run freely along the curved track and past

Our maiden sail in May with trial horse "Nereus" in the background. The goose hung high.

the switch. Had there been more time we probably could have perfected it, but the first trials were fast approaching and we couldn't continue messing with refinements.

We also had to abandon a small coffee grinder for the main. It was slower than trimming by hand when there was little strain and not sufficiently powerful in the latter stages of trimming. Besides, it got in the way and produced high weight and windage. We therefore decided to trim by hand (poor Fenny) and then go to a compact Barient No. 28 for the final trim.

Despite these and other problems, we were growing confident to the point of cockiness as we walloped *Nereus* day after day. One note of caution should have sobered us, and that was the day we practiced starts against Briggs Cunningham sailing *Nereus* with Eric at *Constellation*'s helm. The old dark boat was usually on top of us at the start.

Not the way to lower spinnaker but the way we sometimes did in May. A far cry from September. ↓

An early foulup—not the jib in the water, done on purpose to expedite the spinnaker set. But that sleeve tangled on the clew is bad. It kept giving trouble and later was abandoned as a noble experiment which didn't quite make it.

Eric didn't seem perturbed, however, though I never could understand why we spent so little time practicing this key evolution, especially when the one drill we did have had found us wanting.

Later events showed how important it would have been to practice starts. We had a real advantage in having a trial horse and a keen starter to duel with, yet did so only once before the June series. It was a grave, almost disastrous error, somewhat camouflaged at the time by the fact that even though we were often behind at the start, it was never long before we were ahead of *Nereus.*

This lulled us into a false sense of security. "Bring on *Eagle, Nefertiti* and *Columbia.* We're ready for them." How wrong can you be!

Power and speed. Note the absence of a quarter wave. Bring on "American Eagle", "Nefertiti" and "Columbia". We are ready.

We Race—and Lose

THE SPRING REGATTA of the New York Yacht Club on June 6 gave us the chance to show our stuff. *Eagle* looked sleek and fast even towing out to the line from Luders Shipyard. But as we arrived at the mid-Sound starting line about the same time from Oyster Bay, we felt pretty fast, too. Just let us at them!

There was a beautiful 14-knot southerly blowing—just right for a fair test. Even before the warning signal, I could see Bill Cox working into a position to tail us, and so warned Eric. "I would just as soon be tailed," he replied, much to my surprise. I found a bit of my confidence ebbing as I eyed *Eagle*'s fine-looking main and watched her respond to Cox's well-conceived attack.

And tailed we were, but found refuge in the Committee boat, making tight circles around it with *Eagle* not 30 feet astern of us. With 1½ minutes to go, *Eagle* broke it off, ran off to leeward and came storming back to the line just as we completed our last loop of the Committee boat. She was tight under our leeward bow and in a position to push us over early if we didn't do something. "Kill," shouted Eric with 20 seconds to go, and then "Trim!" as we fell in behind *Eagle*, going at least a knot slower than she. We found out right then that it took *Constellation* a long time to get her main trimmed flat, partly because of our small winch and partly because we failed to advise the crew that only a few seconds remained, and hence the urgency of trimming fast was not realized fully.

We crossed in ignominious fashion with a big luff in the main and badly backwinded by *Eagle*. She was waiting for our tack and tacked with us so that we wound up bow to bow, with *Eagle* one and a half lengths to windward. Now we had our wind clear, though, and could go to work. We soon found we were not racing *Nereus*. Maybe *Eagle* was getting the puffs first, maybe it was because they had eased their main traveler (a fact I was too slow to notice). In any event, it was not long before she had driven off and ahead, not so far as to constitute a foul but enough to put her squarely on our wind.

A series of tacks failed to get us any closer. Instead, *Eagle* continued to gain slightly and finally rounded Oak Neck buoy 40 seconds ahead. The next leg was a beam reach. *Eagle* started off under genoa and we cracked on a spinnaker. Within minutes it was apparent we were right and were gaining fast. As they hurried to follow suit, our guy hopped the cam jam cleat, the sail shot out to leeward about 10 feet and before we had it two-blocked again had lost more than we had gained. This was the same trouble we had experienced in practice with our jibing method.

We held even the rest of the leg, rounding 1 minute, 2 seconds behind, lost on the broad reach down to Noroton, possibly because our main was trimmed wider. Bill made a wide approach and started upwind with the mark tucked in mere feet to weather. Our rounding 1 minute, 38 seconds later was tight at first, then wide, which put us to leeward of *Eagle's* wake. The beat home was dreary, as *Eagle* matched tacks with us, camped all over us and won going away by 2 minutes, 44 seconds. The entry in our log ended with the words "not encouraging."

We had looked bad. Not slow but bad. We felt the wind had favored the leading boat upwind and hence hoped we were justified in feeling our speed was equal to *Eagle* even though she had opened up a bit. On the reaching legs, however, she seemed to have a small but definite edge. One race was enough to tell us it would be a long, hot summer.

Next day was more of the same, except that *Columbia* joined us to make a three-boat race. Eric made a nicely timed run for the line, just to leeward and ahead of *Columbia*, but Bill ruined it by tacking on our leeward bow and crossing again in a beautiful safe leeward. This time it was blowing 8 knots, and once we had tacked and gotten our wind clear, we sailed for 2 miles as if glued together, one length apart. An encouraging note was the way we left *Columbia*. When *Columbia* tacked, we let her go, hoping vainly that *Eagle* would soon tack to cover her and give us clear air.

Dunny and I urged tacking before the lay line so we could later get our wind clear by short tacking, but Eric felt Bill would eventually go for the mark a bit short and we could then get clear air. He was right on that, but after *Eagle* tacked, we had to go a couple of lengths further into flatter air and less favorable current. Result—10 minutes later *Columbia* was first, *Eagle* second and *Constellation* 500 further yards back and a dirty last.

Columbia unaccountably failed to consolidate, and we rounded the same distance behind *Eagle* and in second place. We split jibes on the ensuing dead run and picked the right one, closing to within two lengths of *Eagle* when we reached the next mark. We now know that it wasn't just the fact we picked a better course. *Constellation* could fly on a run and this was the first demonstration of her ability. We carried spinnaker on the reach home and were closing fast at the end, but still 19 seconds back.

In the post-mortem that evening, it was agreed that we were moving well and had seemed at least a match for *Eagle* in the speed department. Get us on top at the start, we felt, and it would be a different outcome. Alas, more easily said than done against Cox.

In a way, these two defeats had been good for us. They didn't count toward selection, we had learned a bit more about trimming and we realized full well that we would have to sharpen up all around if we hoped to win. It was quite different from those carefree days of hosing *Nereus*.

Ev Morris's headline next day in the *New York Herald Tribune* read "*Eagle* Takes the Wind Out of *Constellation*'s Sails." You've never been more right, Ev.

We were an unsmiling group two days later as the first race of the preliminary trials began. These trials were intended more for training than anything else and supposedly didn't count. We didn't altogether buy this and approached them with an eye for blood. The boat entering the later trials with the best record was bound to have an edge with the Selection Committee, and certainly had a psychological advantage. We aimed to have both. Again we were doomed to disappointment.

I'll spare you all the gory details of the next six days, hitting only the high spots or, more accurately, "low spots."

The trials started auspiciously when we met *Columbia* in an 8-knot wind. We took her at the start, ate out upwind, outran her, outreached her, outhandled her and won by over a mile. This was a well-needed tonic because the next day we were to meet *American Eagle*. Our earlier overconfidence was gone, yet I honestly felt we had an even chance to win. This time we used our Hard two-ply main. We had tried the Hood in our first two meetings with *Eagle* and felt its leech was too tight. The Hard had performed handsomely in the light air win over *Columbia*, and we hoped for the same in the 11–12 knots of this day.

Eric got a good start to leeward of *Eagle*, both boats on the line, both with clear air. We held even or perhaps gained almost up to the lay line. But finally we had to tack and had to bear off and go under. When *Eagle* tacked to weather, we had a fine chance but muffed it by squeezing up too soon. We almost backwinded her, but instead she eased by and rounded two lengths ahead.

We made a slow spinnaker set due to faulty communication with Freddy, who was hoisting from below decks. Then when it was hoisted, the cam jams on our jibing line slipped. By the time we were squared away, *Eagle* had jumped us by 150 yards.

We got it all back on the run and rounded the leeward mark only two lengths behind. The ensuing close fetch, from 32A to Cowes, however, cooked us because we had to eat backwind or be blanketed the entire distance. We finally lost by over a minute, but this time had looked at least as fast as *Eagle*. Mistakes in handling, trim and in methods had cost us dearly. When would Cox make a few?

Next day we took on *Nefertiti* in a 15-knot nor'wester, again using our two-ply main. She edged us at the start, but our wind was clear on her leeward bow. A header gave us the lead, we played the shifts well thereafter, seemed to go well and opened out both upwind and down, to win by a comfortable margin. For once in the post-mortem Olin and Rod Stephens, who had been watching, had little criticism and felt we had clearly outsailed a tough adversary. This should have warned us that we had won in spite of the two-ply main, not because of it. It hadn't looked too hot, but we concluded that it was delivering anyway.

That was the last bright spot of the week. Next day in light air, and carrying the Hood main, we met *Columbia*. We led at the start, fell behind when *Columbia* got a private slant, passed her downwind, led by 1½ minutes at the second weather mark with only a 5-mile spinnaker reach to the finish. The wind had been so light that there was less than forty minutes left to finish before the time limit expired and it was nip and tuck whether we could complete the 5 miles in time to make it a race. A good wind had come in, however, and we had hopes of making it and took what we figured was the fastest course for the finish.

This lovely shot typifies the close racing we ran into in the preliminary trials. "Nefertiti" to windward.

When *Columbia* drove off to leeward, we let her go on the theory that if we covered it might cause us to miss the time limit. Imagine our chagrin when *Columbia* came roaring through at the line, beating us by 7 seconds and the clock by 30 seconds! We were just plain stupid to race the clock instead of our opposition, as it would have been far better to have been ahead when time expired than run the risk of losing.

We had carried more hook in the top of the mast, thus easing the leech, and both Dunny and I felt that the Hood main was now our best and that it was handling, not boat speed, which had done us in.

The race next day against *American Eagle* gave us a glimmer of hope, then dashed it. We used Hard sails throughout in the 6-knot breeze. Both boats were even at the start, with us to leeward, a position which favored us when the wind freed and made the intended beat a close reach. We moved very well and led by three lengths at the mark, threw it away by setting too heavy a chute on the next spinnaker reach. We also got our sleeve fouled aloft and Buddy had to be hoisted in a bosun's chair to retrieve it. Approaching the second mark, we were right on *Eagle*'s tail and a snappy jibe might have gained us an overlap. Instead the jibing wire got jammed and we made a fine botch of it, the third time our jibing method had done us in. It was a reach around thereafter, with *Eagle* feeding into better breeze first and continually opening out.

We had lost because of poor judgment on the spinnaker, because we luffed when we should have driven for the mark on the second leg, and because of botching a key jibe. We had lost, and lost decisively, despite a seeming edge in boat speed when both boats had the same wind.

The next morning before the final match in these trials, against *Nefertiti*, Dunny and I had a conference. We decided I should be more decisive in recommending tactics. Dunny was to let me know his thoughts and then I was to decide what I thought we should do and whenever I felt strongly was to urge Eric to do it in no uncertain terms. We felt a bit like Monday morning quarterbacks but also felt that few of the tactical errors we had made were of our choice. I assumed much blame for them, however, because I hadn't voiced my views strongly enough. We decided to stick our necks well out in the future and speak our minds.

Next day we lost the first round, however, when it came to selecting sails. It was blowing 20 knots and Dunny and I felt our best chances lay with our Hood. Eric favored the Hard, based, I suppose, on our big win over *Columbia* and our decisive beating of *Nefertiti* with it. I argued that the *Columbia* races, however, were in light air and that we had outsailed *Nefertiti* in 12 to 15 knots more on tactics than on speed. Eric prevailed, however, and we used the two-ply main but with a Hood jib we all liked.

Soon after getting an even start, however, it was apparent that we had made a grave error. In the 20-knot wind our main bagged out hopelessly and luffed all the way back to the battens! *Nefertiti* outpointed us alarmingly and outfooted us, too. It looked like a hopeless situation, but two things made it a great boat race. *Nefertiti* broke her coffee grinders and had to use small deck winches to trim her genoa and hence couldn't tack well to cover and couldn't tack as often in the headers as Ted Hood would have liked. I spent the race hovering over the compass and looking for shifts to windward. We kept tacking in them and, having a crippled adversary, were able to keep close despite sailing at considerably slower speed.

On the first run we drew ahead, then lost it by a slow jibe and started upwind half a length behind. *Nefertiti* had repaired her winches and moved away fast. She let us go though on one tack and a wonderful lift brought us back to within half a length at the mark.

It was a real thriller shooting downwind in 25-knot puffs. Finally we drew even and to leeward and, since a jibe was required to make the finish and we could jibe first, we appeared in the driver's seat.

After jibing, we had a length of open water between us as we were heading for the finish 1 mile away. It looked good for a few seconds but we couldn't seat our jibing wire and the tack of the spinnaker was well off to leeward (the fourth time in a week the jibing method had done us in). Before we could winch it home, *Nefertiti* had driven by to windward to win by seven seconds—a real thriller for the spectators, but a crushing blow for us!

Ev Morris's story next day summing up the trials was headlined "*Eagle* Gem of the Ocean." Zander Hollander's story in the *World-Telegram* was captioned "*Constellation* Finds Yacht Trials Tough." Well put, Zander. He went on to say: "The soaring flight of *American Eagle* has been in marked contrast to that of *Constellation*, a relative pigeon in the just concluded first set of America's Cup trials. . . . One fact emerges against all others: Skipper Cox and his crew have left the others astern."

As if we had to be told! Our record in the trials was 2 wins, 4 losses—same as both *Columbia* and *Nefertiti*. *Eagle*'s was 6–0. Counting the two New York Yacht Club races, our record to date was 2–6, while *Eagle*'s was 8–0.

We found that everyone we talked to, while making brave efforts to be polite, found it impossible to hide their conviction that *Eagle* was home free and that while more important and longer trials lay ahead, they were merely a formality, with *Eagle*'s eventual selection virtually assured.

We were chastened, to be sure, but not one man on board *Constellation* bought that for a minute. We were just more determined and we had the benefit of knowing a myriad of mistakes we had made which we felt confident we could correct or avoid in the future. I knew we had a crew at least equal to any of them, with the possible exception of the afterguard.

Our post-mortem of mistakes included the following:

1. Leading the spinnaker and jib halyards below had made hoisting

With two miles to go in our second race against "Nefertiti" (No. 19) we appear to have it made. Both boats are sailing by the lee, the finish is off our port bow and we have "Neffie" nicely blocked.

After the jibe we have the lead we anticipated but look at our pole. The jibing wires have jammed and our spinnaker is on its own.

Our pole is now raised and if we can just grind the spinnaker tack down to it before the sail collapses we may be O.K. "Nefertiti" hasn't gained yet.

No luck. Just when we almost had it made the spinnaker collapses. Had the sheet been trimmed along with the guy we might have saved it. "Nefertiti" is boiling.

Snugged down at last but we have lost our wind and our last real hope of winning the race.

It's all over now. We finished this distance behind in a race we should have won. Our advisors look on glumly from "Chaperone's" flying bridge.

slow, had resulted in lack of communication and had necessitated getting one man out of circulation and hence unable to do anything else or jump in on emergencies. Solution: We would move the halyard winches up on deck, thus raising the center of gravity and increasing windage slightly but at a sure improvement in efficiency.

2. The *Windigo* jibing method had probably cost us at least two races and had made us lose ground in others. Solution: Get rid of it once and for all and go to the *Vim* method.

3. The Hard two-ply main, despite frequent recutting, was hopeless in a breeze and no faster than the Hood in light air. Solution: Write it off as a noble experiment that failed, put in the bag forever. Ease the leech on the Hood (plus whatever else Ted might recommend) and use it, or another Hood about to arrive, forever after. We also felt we should stick pretty much to Hood jibs and spinnakers.

4. The spinnaker sleeve had let us down twice. Solution: Go either to zippers on the sail or set flying.

5. Many tactical errors. Solution: I should be more decisive in calling the shots and should be smarter, too.

6. Starts were often poor. Solution: Lots of practice.

7. Often set too heavy and too big a spinnaker. Solution: When in doubt, go to a ¾-ounce chute and lean on smaller ones.

8. Communications were often poor. Solution: Be sure to pass the word and install an intercom between the forward hatch and the cockpit.

If we had not been able to point to so many mistakes, we would have been disconsolate. Suppose, for example, we had sailed really well, and had good sails all the time, yet still had a 2–6 record to show for it. Then we would have been low. Recognizing mistakes and then knowing what to do to avoid them in the future has always been the mark of any good sailor, and despite the many we had made, we took solace in the recognition of them and the belief we could and would correct them.

Therefore as we headed for Newport several days later, while we went with none of the overconfidence with which we entered our first race, we felt no defeatism either. The rest of the sailing world had largely written *Constellation* off, but not a single man on board *Constellation* had. Like John Paul Jones, we had just begun to fight.

We Go to Newport

FOLLOWING THE PRELIMINARY trials, all hands slunk home for a few days. I went to the office each day in a vain effort to complete everything which "just had to be done" before taking off for the summer. Then one last weekend at home on a busman's holiday crewing for my son in our Lightning. (He got second out of fifteen boats.) Far better than the seconds we had been getting!

Eric had passed the word for all hands to arrive in Newport Sunday evening, June 21, so we could start to work bright and early the next day. Everyone was there by 10:00 P.M.

Our home for the summer was Castle Hill—a brown-shingled Victorian hotel which Eric had rented for our exclusive use. It had seen better days, had not seen a decorator in years, but was in sound repair and boasted an ample supply of large bedrooms for the entire crew, our wives, Rod or Olin Stephens and Bill Stiger of Sparkman & Stephens. They were there to advise us and to look after *Constellation*'s needs and to bring her to mechanical perfection.

What charm Castle Hill lacked inside as a building it more than made up for in location. It is situated right next to Castle Hill Lighthouse, from which it derived its name. Directly across from us was Beavertail Lighthouse, marking the entrance to Narragansett Bay. To the north we had a direct view of the entrance to Newport, to the south we looked out to sea on Brenton's Tower. Every vessel entering Newport passed right by us. We had a saluting cannon on the lawn and a fearful supply of blanks which we delighted in using to salute warships and yachts of all descriptions. There was so much land belonging to Castle Hill that no house could be seen—just rolling fields, rocky promontories and the sea beyond. *Gretel's* Australian crew had stayed there in 1962, and we were proud to be their successors.

Staying at Castle Hill was a lot like going back to boarding school. Our life was no longer our own. We had set hours to keep, tight schedules to maintain and precious little personal freedom. The basic difference was that we all wanted to be there, all appreciated the necessity of a team effort to accomplish all we had to do.

Our day started with a violent pound on the door by John Handel, our "drill sergeant," entrusted with getting us in shape. All hands were down on the lawn by 7:15 for 20 minutes of setting-up exercises, followed by a 1-mile run. Due to our relatively sedentary roles and "advanced age," Eric and I were excused, but I elected to do it. I often regretted my decision as I tried vainly to keep up with our athletic twenty-year-olds, but after a month of this was in pretty good shape. Even so, the miles were a lot longer than they used to be when I was in college.

A quick shower and we stormed in to a big breakfast at 8:00 and were down at the yard by 9:00 ready for sailing, or for the apparently never-ending yard work.

We were usually back at the dock by 6:00 and home at Castle Hill about 7:00. Cocktails were then the order of the day for all who wanted them. We felt this training business could be carried too far, and I for one was ready to smash anyone who didn't think the two drinks I had

Setting up exercises started the normal day at Castle Hill. Only on race days were we excused. ↓

The favorite pastime at our huge breakfasts (next to eating) was reading what the newspapers said about us and our competition.

"Constellation's" summer home was alongside "Chaperone" at the end of the Newport Shipyard dock. Here the boat bath is being removed prior to getting underway.

We practiced jibes by the hour prior to the July trials. Everyone got to know their jobs so well that hardly a word was spoken.

each evening were not a sound idea. Despite the fact there was no precise limit on the dividends one could pour, I never saw any crew member get the least bit high at Castle Hill, with the notable exception of those great days in September following our selection and the last race against *Sovereign*.

It was often close to 9:00 when we were through dinner, a dinner attended usually by all hands. Wives were there but dates were verboten except on rare occasions. After dinner the talk was usually sailing, sometimes small talk for fun, sometimes a serious huddle going over the day's mistakes or the plans for the next day. Briggs Cunningham, Jerry Driscoll, Rod, Olin or Bill Stiger would often join us for these discussions, and their observations were of great help. If you liked to talk sailing, had set your sights on one all-consuming goal, these evenings were fun. If you were a well-rounded person, interested in what went on in the world at large, they would be sure to bore you. The fact that I enjoyed them thoroughly and never got bored or stir-crazy really stamped me. Charlotte used to marvel at the fact that a group of active men could be not only content but could thrive on such a narrow existence. The fact that most of us did shows what fanatics we were.

Curfew was at 11:00 and 10:00 on race days, hours which for most were no hardship. Just how our young bucks were able to get back from a date by that hour was hard to figure, and there were times when they didn't. An occasional breaking of curfew was overlooked, but if repeated too often, the offender was given a quiet talk, the gist of which was to ask him what he was there for.

The most serious complaint came over girls—or rather no girls. The bachelors were expected to eat with us most evenings, and since the presence of girls was discouraged even after dinner, and since that curfew was always there, it was no mean job to get a date. Charlotte and I were all for more social life at Castle Hill, but Eric held out against it on the basis, I guess, of keeping the crew's mind strictly on *Constellation*. Our eventual success would indicate that he might have been right but I never felt that having a few girls around would have lost us the America's Cup, and they sure would have been great morale builders.

Our days afloat were so full that there was never any morale problem, no chance to get bored once we left the dock. Getting under way, however, was often a problem. I doubt if there ever was a better-built boat than *Constellation*, yet the yard work required almost every morning and evening was staggering. The hull never needed any work done on it other than normal polishing, but our designing team was busy devising or ordering new fittings, relocating old ones, adjusting and modifying rigging, installing winch handle holders in locations where they proved most handy, adding anti-foul guards for all cleats, and repairing damage. One day our stainless steel gooseneck pin would be found to have developed a bend. Bill Stiger, Rod or Olin would design a new one on the spot and within an hour a custom-made replacement would be ordered. We found the backstay whips were eating into our aluminum drum winches. Solution—continue the stainless steel facing on the drum to extend ¾ inch down onto the curved base. Cost—$300 per drum; saving—about 10 pounds over going to readily available all-steel drums. Attention to scores of minor details such as this added up to a significant improvement in speed or ease of handling.

Newport Shipyard did a great job. When we arrived in the morning, their gang would already be well along on the jobs ordered but not completed the previous evening. More important, perhaps than their technical know-how, was their enthusiasm. They appeared to harbor no doubts about *Constellation*'s ultimate victory and backed up their opinion by betting their overtime pay with the gang at Williams and Manchester, where *American Eagle* was being cared for. Their continued good humor and confidence made us feel great but also were a bit frightening. Here we had never beaten *American Eagle*, yet the Newport Shipyard workers were so confident that we would, they were backing us with cold cash. We felt we had to win for that gang.

We didn't rely on the yard for maintenance of our gear. Keeping winches, rigging and equipment in top shape was our responsibility. Dick Goennel was appointed as bosun to direct all maintenance work. He did it with a smile, but he also got the work done so well that failure or malfunction of our equipment became a thing of the past.

Once clear of the dock, our days really came alive. Though we did it every day for months on end, I never ceased to get a kick out of hoisting sail and then feeling our beautiful boat heel to the wind and knife her way through the seas. Day after day Briggs Cunningham, the America's Cup winning skipper on *Columbia* in 1958, would take *Nereus* out to brush with us. He often had Jerry Driscoll, a West Coast boatbuilder, with him. Jerry had won the Star World's Championship some years ago and had since been cleaning up in ocean racers on the West Coast. He was sharp and determined to do all he could to help us get sharp too, both afloat and through helping in yard work.

Much of our time was spent checking sails. We would try one headsail against *Nereus*, then switch to another and try to determine which performed better. The fact that *Constellation* was faster no matter what sails we carried made the evaluation difficult, but we could still tell something. We also shifted mains and spinnakers, and as the days wore on, we got to know our sails very well, learned exactly which one was better than another, and in what wind range.

Indicative of the importance of sails was the fact that when we used our two-ply main, we were barely able to beat *Nereus*—an encouraging discovery, since this was the sail we had used so much in the June trials.

The sail-testing process took longer because of frequent recutting. Invariably our sails became better after recutting, and this made it necessary to evaluate them all over again. We ordered very few new sails, feeling it was better to recut ones we already had in hopes of making them even better. Having few sails helped us know the ones we did have and insured having the right one up for the conditions in hand.

While we relied on *Nereus* to test sails against, we had a secret weapon for determining the best trim and weight distribution. It was a novel speedometer developed by a couple of sharp young engineers—Dick Condon and Mal Redmond. In addition to the usual 5-knot and 10-knot scale, it had a 1-knot scale. To make it work, after switching to the 1-knot scale, one would adjust the pointer to the midpoint of the dial (5 knots). Let's assume speed prior to switching to that scale was 7 knots. If the pointer went down to 0, this meant a loss of ½ knot, or a speed of 6½ knots. If it went up to 10, it indicated an actual speed of 7½ knots. This meant that it was possible to detect speed variations of one hundredth of a knot! The instrument was beautifully dampened to remove the momentary effect of hitting a sea and to average out speed changes. With it we could ease the main traveler 3 inches and see a change in speed. Or we could adjust crew location forward or aft by just a foot or two and see the difference. To insure that the different reading was a result of change in trim or weight and not because of a sudden change in wind or steering, we would make the change again and again, perhaps ten times in quick succession, by which time a definite pattern would be established. We would then record in our sail book the optimum point of traveler adjustment for a given weight of wind or the best crew location for different conditions.

We never used the 1-knot scale in a race because we couldn't then make the necessary repeated adjustments, but it earned its keep in telling us what precise trim was best, prior to the start of a race.

In addition to testing sails, trim and weight distribution, we went through evolutions by the hour. We would beat out 7 or 8 miles, making several jib changes en route, checking the time each change took by stop watch. They got faster almost every day. Then we would set spinnaker, make say fifteen jibes in quick succession. The *Vim* method proved wonderful, and it wasn't long before a muffed jibe was one in which the spinnaker broke for even a second. Almost invariably it stayed hard full throughout the evolution. Dunny was a great one for adding realism to these drills by picking buoys to jibe around or to douse at. We enjoyed these drills because of the satisfaction of seeing ourselves getting better.

We tried carrying spinnaker right up to a mark, jibing, taking it down on the new leeward side just as we were in the very act of rounding and then seeing how soon we could tack without being entirely fouled up. It never ceased to amaze me, after a couple of weeks of this drill, to hear a shout from the foredeck—"You can tack now"—when the stern had barely cleared the mark. We would tack on cue, the jib would come around, trailing sheets and guys with it, to be sure, but still with no delay in getting sheeted home. Then all deck hands would swarm around clearing up the mess so we could tack back. We were to use this drill to great effect in months to come.

One maneuver we never used in a race but which we were saving for a crucial moment was jibing with the spinnaker staysail set. Accepted practice was always to lower the spinnaker staysail prior to a jibe and, in fact, it is generally believed to be impossible for the pole to swing through the foretriangle unless the staysail is lowered. Dick Goennel, however, thought it might be accomplished, and what a great advantage of surprise this would give. If two boats were neck and neck and one could jibe 10 seconds before another, it could mean the boat race. When one lowers her spinnaker staysail, however, it is a signal to the other that a jibe is coming up and so she lowers staysail too, and gets ready. Since it takes perhaps 10 seconds to lower staysail and get it out of the pole's way, jibing with it up could really leave your opponent flatfooted. We tried it, therefore, casting off the sheet and halyard just as the pole swung through. To our amazement we found the jibe could be made without a hitch. True the spinnaker staysail would end up plastered against the pole, but it was a relatively simple matter to clear up immediately after the jibe. It was a real regret we never had an opportunity to spring this one. Twelve-Meter crews pride themselves on watching every action of the other boat in order to be able to respond instantly, and it would have been a real shock to our opponent to see us jibe in a condition which they considered impossible.

In my opinion the most important drill we did was practicing starts against *Nereus*, followed some of the time by a short brush to windward. The first time we did this against Briggs Cunningham, Jerry Driscoll coached Briggs and I talked things over with Eric, who was at *Constellation*'s wheel. Honors were approximately even, with perhaps a slight edge in *Nereus*'s favor.

To my delight, Eric suggested the next day that henceforth I shift over to *Nereus* and sail her in these brushes. I felt a little presumptuous being ferried over in the Bertram which was accompanying us and then relieving a former America's Cup skipper of the wheel. Briggs, however, took it all in stride and never for a moment appeared the least bit resentful. He was giving up his summer to be of assistance to us in any way he could and with no personal ambitions. He had had his licks in 1958 and acquitted himself admirably.

To make things fairer, Briggs was directed not to give advice during the starts, though his criticism afterward would be more than welcome. Jerry Driscoll was to be my second pair of eyes and my advisor. We got along famously and he was so much on the ball, so sharp that it would surprise me not at all to see him skipper of a Cup candidate in 1967.

The first day I practiced starts against *Constellation* was an exhilarating experience to me and apparently to all hands on *Nereus*. Not so on Constellation. We made seven starts and I managed to take five of them clearly. The gang on *Nereus* got so excited they started pasting Kenyon tape X marks on our blue topsides, indicating the number of "kills." I guess I was swept up in the excitement too, because I let them do it.

I figured this one day's success might have been beginner's luck, but the pattern was similar day after day. The second day the *Nereus* crew started pasting "kill" marks on again, but I quickly squashed that. We were there to sharpen Eric up, not to have a personal contest. Eric seemed not a bit put out by the one-sidedness of these starts and in fact appeared unconcerned and almost oblivious of the fact that more often than not, he was coming out second best.

A number of *Constellation*'s crew congratulated me in private. Their public recognition of my growing status in their eyes was a new nickname, "Reynard," coined by Dunny but picked up by all hands. It was, I must admit, not only flattering but enjoyable to me to be so called, but I found myself getting quite uncomfortable at the same time. I felt sure that Eric would continue to start *Constellation*, yet it was disquieting to the crew and to me to see that he could be beaten quite often. Each night we would discuss the starts with Jerry, Briggs and I advising countermeasures to the best of our ability, yet the next day the score, while never unanimous and sometimes close, would be in our favor.

Just a few days before the July trials and at the conclusion of our last starting practice, Eric suggested we try one more start, then race 2½ miles to windward to one of the torpedo range buoys and then 7½ miles back into the harbor. On *Nereus* we knew it would take a real jump at the start for us to have any chance of beating *Constellation* for a 10-mile course. We got particularly aggressive, therefore, managed to block *Constellation* away from the line and crossed two lengths ahead and directly on her wind. Our blanketing was so effective that she was eight lengths back before she got clear air. By later leaving her and tacking first for the mark, we still had the same lead as we rounded and headed downwind. I realized we could never hold our lead, however, with orthodox tactics on the run home and hence instead of covering tacked downwind in the light wind then prevailing. It worked and we "won" by several hundred yards.

This mock race, of course, didn't prove much because in a real race Eric doubtless would have followed us, relying on his greater speed to get by. I'm sure his more direct course was dictated by a desire to learn the relative advantage of running vs. tacking downwind in that weight of wind. Still it wasn't good for morale for our skipper to be beaten by *Nereus* even in a fun race, and I found my initial exuberance at beating that great boat and great crew quickly waning as I realized the morale problem it could cause.

My success in these starts and in that one mock race, however, did have a very beneficial result. It gave me the confidence and assurance to speak out in my capacity as tactician and advisor and I suspected that it helped Eric to look at me with greater respect and to take advice with even greater willingness. Both of us had learned a great deal from brushing against each other, and now that we would be racing henceforth as a team we should make a highly effective one. At least that was our fervent hope as *Constellation* was hauled for final polishing before the July trials which began on the eighth. We knew we had come a long way in the last two weeks. We knew our boat was going faster, knew our techniques of handling were now sound and that we were operating as a smooth team with the days of experiments long behind us. We had entered the June trials a pretty cocky bunch. There was none of that now. We could see *Eagle* out practicing each day and knew they were getting sharper, too. We could not dismiss *Nefertiti* and her keen crew and on a given day *Columbia* and *Easterner* could be rough.

The magazine press had already selected *American Eagle*. There were feature articles in big circulation magazines. *Eagle* even made the *Saturday Evening Post* front cover, and her picture seemed to crop up everywhere. We could see photographers snapping her every move, from helicopters, boats and from the dock. Editors had given instructions to get a full file on the next America's Cup defender, and how could it be other than the boat which never had lost a race?

Even the *New York Times* shared the popular view and, on the record, who could blame them? On the eve of the July trials, an article was captioned "American Eagle Is Expected to Gain Defender's Role." It then continued: "If Las Vegas oddsmakers booked for the America's Cup, the price on *American Eagle* and Bill Cox to win that prize would be a short one, like 4 to 5."

Hardly reassuring things to see, hear and read but, while recognizing our underdog role, I felt we had the fastest boat, knew we had made great strides in handling and techniques and felt that if we sailed as well as Bill Cox and his crew, we would fool an awful lot of people. Were we just fooling ourselves? The ten days starting July 8 would tell the story.

The July Trials

Improvement but Frustration

O N THE SUNDAY before the July trials, I joined Eric at the skippers' meeting. There we received instructions from the Race Committee, all very basic, and drew lots for the pairings. We drew *Easterner* for the first race, followed by *Nefertiti*, *Columbia* and finally *American Eagle*. Good! That would give us three lesser tests before the big one against the boat we knew we had to beat.

Our confidence had been rebuilt to the point we were quite sure we could handle the three older boats but not to the point that we didn't want all possible practice before tackling Bill Cox.

These races were termed Observation Trials, indicating that the Selection Committee would be paying strict attention. True, they would count less than the Selection Trials in August, but we all knew a good showing here would help our cause.

The first race against *Easterner* in moderate weather was like taking candy from a baby. The only excitement was at the start when Eric forced Charlie Hovey over the line early, but in the process got us over too. We recovered first and led throughout, widening out both upwind and down. It was painful to look at *Easterner*'s tired-looking old sails, but we were thankful not to have to suffer from similar lack of equipment. The margin at the end was well over a mile in distance and 14 minutes, 51 seconds in time—the worst defeat any Twelve had ever inflicted on another in trials or races for the Cup itself. *Eagle* also walloped *Columbia*, while *Nefertiti* sat it out. Ev Morris's heading in the *Tribune* next day told the story, "*Constellation, Eagle* Defeat Two Old Ladies."

Next day it was blowing fresh for our meeting with *Nefertiti*—weather she reveled in two years before. We felt this could be a stern test against Ted Hood and his very able crew, and we were not far wrong. We tried our No. 2 main, not knowing at that time that the No. 1 was a bit better in a breeze. Eric got a good even start, two lengths to leeward of *Nefertiti*. Within 10 minutes we had squeezed up and forced her about. Thereafter we slowly but inexorably drew away to lead by just over a minute after 9 miles of beating. We opened further on the run, lost a few seconds on a close reach home to win by 1 minute, 26 seconds. Not a smashing win, but a good one considering it was *Nefertiti*'s best weather—25 knots at the finish. We felt pretty good.

We felt still better next day when we slaughtered *Columbia* by nearly 8 minutes in a 22-knot breeze, on a windward, leeward, windward, leeward, windward course. The sea was smooth, since the Observation Trials were being held inshore of the America's Cup course, and with a northerly wind our first leg took us right in to Beavertail.

Eric caught Walter Podolak barging at the start, squeezed him out at the last instant and by the time he had tacked and jibed, we were more than a minute ahead. Thereafter we both outpointed and outfooted *Columbia* upwind, opened up more downwind and in general ate her up. The No. 1 main we used looked particularly good and we concluded it was better at least in a breeze than the No. 2 we had used in beating *Nefertiti* the day before.

The goose hung high at Castle Hill that night. I was particularly pleased that in three starts we had been even in two and had taken the third. Our spinnaker handling had been crisp, our tacking had gone

Our chief rivals and early favorites, the crew of "American Eagle". (Left to right, front row) Dick Walling, George Hinman, Jr., Bill Cox, Tom Hovey, Dooie Isdale. (Back row) Kevin Garvey, Dave Gundy, Halsey Herreshoff, Bob Barton, Robby Robinson, Bill Stetson, John Nichols, Dick MacNamara.

"Nefertiti's" crew got the most out of her. (Left to right): Bruce Hood, Sted Amory, Don Logan, John Osgood, Dave Rockerfeller, Glit Shields, Jon Wales, Toby Cosgrove, Warwick Tompkins, Ross Anderson, Jr., Ted Hood. (Not pictured) Mike Deland, Ken Burns, Tex Mason, Steve Wales and Jeff Montgomery.

Californians all, the popular crew of "Columbia". (Left to right): Bill Lilly, Bill Lawhorn, Rob Dougan, Jack Hart, Pat Dougan, Fred MacDonald, Herb Riley, Tom Dougan, John Gettle, Don Vaughn, Walter Podolak, Ron Young.

"Easterner" appeared a bit tired but not her young crew. (Left to right): Sammy Wakeman, Rick Wakeman, Ben Hovey, Sam Wakeman, Sherman Morss, Pat Morss, Jon Millar, Charles Hovey, Jr., Steve Connett, Charles Francis, Charlie Hovey, Bee Hovey.

well and, all in all, we looked and felt like a different boat from the one which limped through the preliminary races. The only rub was that *American Eagle* had looked equally impressive and had yet to lose. We had at least established ourselves as a real contender and, like the baseball writers who preview a midseason meeting of two leading teams as a crucial game, we thought of our meeting with *Eagle* next day as just that. All hands made curfew that night, but whether we all slept well, I don't know. I did, accompanied by some pleasant dreams in which I kept looking *back* at a boat which looked surprisingly like *American Eagle.*

It was a beautiful sailing day when we reached the start near Brenton's Tower—about 12 knots, with the likelihood of more and a warm sun. We chose a 9-ounce jib and our No. 1 main.

In the prestart maneuvering, *Eagle* got on our tail, but with 3½ minutes to go and heading away from the windward end of the line, we just had room to tack. Though this would put us early for the windward end, Bill tacked inside and to leeward of us. For an instant we had an opportunity to swing *Eagle's* stern and go to leeward. This would enable us to keep heading for the line. We hesitated momentarily, and as *Eagle* killed way we became overlapped on her windward side with the line on her leeward bow. "Now the fat's in the fire," I thought, "but how to get out of it?" There were 3½ minutes to go and we were about 1 minute from the line. If we tried to pass to windward, *Eagle* would surely go with us and luff us wide at the line, dipping back first to cross and getting away well in the lead. If we tacked with the intention of later jibing, *Eagle* would doubtless follow suit and keep us blocked from the line. The best chance seemed to lie in killing way in hopes of being able to swing under her stern and go for it.

We shot head to the wind. *Eagle* followed. We luffed jib and main. So did *Eagle.* We backed the jib. *Eagle* backed hers. And after a minute of this we were just where we started—30 feet to windward and with our bow abreast the forward end of her cockpit.

"What do you suggest, Bob?" asked Eric. "Shall we try tacking?" "Too late," I replied. "We've had it. Let's plan to cross right in their wake and tack at the mark. In that way we will be close anyway and should get clear air." Eric agreed readily, largely because I'm sure he had come to the same conclusion. This was no time to try anything desperate which might really put us out of it.

With 45 seconds remaining, Cox trimmed down and reached for the buoy at the windward end of the line. We followed suit, falling in directly astern and as close as we could come without running up on her counter. *Eagle* was 15 seconds late at the gun. A perfect start, since we were 25 seconds late.

We tacked at the mark but *Eagle*, of course, was ready and tacked with us. We wound up bow to bow a length and a half to leeward. Not good, but not bad if we could now go. Eric, however, went hard on the wind and Cox drove as much as the rule would allow. By the time we started driving too, it was too late and she was on top of us. Even so, we hung on grimly through a number of tacks and rounded the weather mark only 30 seconds behind.

We were the same distance back when we started upwind again, this time with a 5-ounce jib in lieu of the 9-ounce, the wind having failed to build as we anticipated, and this time we actually gained despite Cox's careful covering. We were only three lengths behind as we started the run for home. It wasn't over yet by a long shot.

Eagle went off on starboard tack and we picked the port jibe. It was soon apparent that ours was working and we couldn't understand why Bill didn't jibe over to cover. We later found that his guy was fouled and he couldn't jibe. Had we only known at the time, we could have camped all over him. It didn't seem to matter, however, because our jibe was clearly best, and with just 3 miles to go, we seemed definitely ahead. We had to jibe eventually for the finish and hence debated jibing when we felt we were leading. We didn't for fear of coming in just ahead and being blanketed and also because we seemed in a better spot than *Eagle*, anyway. It was in direct violation of the axiom "when ahead in a match race, cover." This is true on a run as well as upwind, and we soon lived to regret our decision.

Just as we reached the point to jibe for the line, the wind hauled and gave us a dead run for the finish. *Eagle* had jibed by this time, and as soon as the new wind reached her, she had a gorgeous reach for the line. We eventually jibed for it but knew immediately that we were dead, since *Eagle*'s bearing kept drawing ahead. She finally crossed 54 seconds ahead. Damn!

Our log reading concluded, "Our speed at least equal." Actually it was, in my opinion, superior. Bill had simply sailed a better race. Encouraging but discouraging, too. We felt more than ever that our boat was equal to the task. But were we?

The next two races did nothing to bolster our confidence in ourselves. We had a lay day July 12 and raced *Easterner* on July 13 in a 15–20-knot wind—*Easterner* weather. We were very late at the start, at least three lengths behind, but *Constellation* bailed us out, with some help from *Easterner*. We tacked more smoothly and our great crew sheeted us home faster, so that after 3 miles we were even and with clear air. Then *Easterner*'s jib halyard parted. We went on to win by 3 minutes, 45 seconds. Even without *Easterner*'s gear failure we would surely have won, but we hadn't looked good and I felt we never would have caught *American Eagle* after such a licking at the start.

That evening in a private huddle with Eric, I queried whether it might be smart if I took a crack at starting and sailing part of the time thereafter. I hesitated to suggest it, but this seemed like no time for being a shrinking violet even though I was leery if I could do as well or better with such limited experience. Eric evidently was doubtful, too, but said he would consider it and when and if he felt such a move was best for *Constellation* would be the first to suggest it. Except for the last two he had sailed some pretty good races in these trials and, like any good sailor, he had considerable self-confidence. Quite frankly I did too and felt that there were times when *Constellation* was not being sailed quite up to her potential. Whether I could either was questionable, but with summer half over and *Eagle* still undefeated, it seemed time to try *something*. I could well appreciate, however, how hard it would be for Eric, after his months of superb organizing and zealous practice, to turn the wheel over to someone less experienced for a critical phase of a race, and I began to feel sorry I had opened my big mouth. Eric seemed in no way to have resented my suggestion, and our personal relationship was as friendly as ever.

It remained friendly in the next race, in the most trying circumstances. The race scheduled against *Nefertiti* July 14 was called for lack of wind and on July 15 for fog, but the 16th dawned clear, with a nice moderate wind. That was one of the few bright spots of the day. Ted Hood got on our tail, blocked us from jibing or tacking back to the line, and when time had run out, went for it with *Constellation* following lamely in his wake—but not so lame as met the eye. We decided to tack as soon as we passed the Committee boat, just as we had when *Eagle* took us two races before. Mindful of the need to get clear air

The beautiful "Columbia", America's Cup defender in 1958, was not a serious contender in '64. The lessons learned will make her a threat in the 1967 trials. →

"Nefertiti" and "Easterner". "Easterner" usually got good starts but couldn't hang on thereafter and lost each race she entered. ↓

upon tacking, Eric cut the Committee boat close. Too close! We grazed it as we swept by, to groans from the crew. We were out of the race before it really began. Eric and I took just a second to agree to race anyway and drop out at the finish. We tacked and got our wind clear despite the first sluggish trimming our crew had done all spring and summer. "Com'on, you guys," I shouted. "Let's beat 'em before we drop out." From then on our crew work was as efficient as ever but unsmiling and without their usual bounce.

Eric knuckled down, and two thirds of the way up the leg and after seven or eight tacks, we were ahead and apparently in the driver's seat. "If only we could do this to *Eagle*," I thought. But Hood was far from dead. Though several lengths behind at the mark, *Nefertiti* carried her reaching chute beautifully and threatened to go by. We luffed her long enough to make it a jibe for the mark, executed a snappy jibe and had regained our margin at the next mark. The reach to the starting buoy was a bit broader and we added another length, starting upwind nearly 30 seconds ahead. This should be duck soup.

We waited for *Nefertiti* to tack, followed suit on her weather beam and then expected to march out. In a way we did, pointing far higher, but *Nefertiti* was footing well—very well. I expressed concern and said we felt sluggish, but Eric continued to point. Soon it was apparent that we were no better than even, with *Nefertiti* well to leeward but also well out on our lee bow. Then a header and she had us cold.

Thereafter, after tacking, we seemed to go again and halved the distance, but the damage seemed done when *Neffie* rounded 40 seconds ahead with just a run remaining.

By this time we knew *Constellation* loved to run and how she proved it! We first engaged in a jibing duel—some nine or ten jibes in quick succession. Jibes on both boats were good, but we were closing on each one. Finally they muffed one, we got an overlap to leeward with our bow about 10 feet in the lead and the mark dead ahead. So long as we held this position we would win, since we had been tacking downwind and our approach angle favored the leeward boat. Occasionally we would draw ahead, be blanketed momentarily and *Nefertiti* would draw even, but never ahead. There was nothing for us to do but keep sailing and hope she couldn't pass. We couldn't luff her unless we drew clear ahead. For three miles we sailed overlapped less than a length apart and it was during this time which would normally be exciting but which

Start of the most exciting jibing duel of the summer in which we overcame a 40 second deficit against "Nefretiti". Here the pole has just been tripped and the jibe begins.

The pole is swinging down and across, the boat bearing off and the sail remains full. Buddy in the bow prepares to snap the guy in as the pole swishes by.

somehow seemed to lack something, that Eric—who had sailed every foot of the way—turned to me and said, quietly and matter-of-factly: "Tomorrow you start." The poor guy had been eating his heart out over our foul, and over letting *Nefertiti* catch us and wanted me to know then and now, and irrespective of whether we crossed first, that referring to our conversation of several nights before, he felt the time had come to try something else.

I wish I could have thought of something more worthy of such a tough decision on his part, but instead merely blurted, "O.K., but now let's beat *Nefertiti*." A moment later I realized that what I said was a better reflection of my feelings than I first realized. I wanted, suddenly, very much to get across that line first. Not for *Constellation* this time, since we couldn't win officially, but for Eric.

The timing of Eric's decision is important to remember. A lot of ill-informed people are still under the impression that Eric relinquished *Constellation*'s wheel only as the result of pressure by syndicate members or advisors. Sure there were some suggestions made, some conferences held which at that time I was barely aware of, but Eric was not one to quit under fire. Nor did he quit. He simply made up his *own* mind during three hours of a nip-and-tuck boat race. Dunny heard our brief conversation, but the rest of the crew was too far removed, too busy with the job in hand.

Just before the finish, Ted Hood sharpened up to gather speed. We went halfway with him but kept edging down for the favored end of the line. When he squared off for it, our wind was clear, our bow in front and we got the gun 2 seconds before *Nefertiti* got her whistle. It was the closest "win" in 12-Meter history, a nice companion to the largest margin in history we had achieved in the first race of these July trials.

Normally our crew would have exploded at such a finish. This time they merely went about the business of dousing spinnaker and clearing up lines as we beat back to the Committee boat under main alone. When we got there, Eric called over to the chairman, Briggs Dalzell: "Briggs, obviously we withdraw."

Sailing in, we had the usual post-mortem in the cockpit—shorter than usual despite the fact that we had much we could discuss. No one seemed very talkative. At the end, almost as if it was an afterthought, Eric said, "By the way, Bob will start against *Eagle* tomorrow."

The connection is made, the main is being horsed in and the guy is about to be trimmed. "Nefertiti" prepares to follow suit.

The main flops over, the pole is raised, the guy trimmed and sheet adjusted. "Nefertiti's" pole has started its dizzy swing down.

Jibe almost complete now. We exert a bit of blanketing as we cross "Nefertiti's" stern. Time from first shot in sequence about 8 seconds.

"Nefertiti" has just completed her jibe but we are already jibing back. They will follow as fast as possible. Distance closing.

"Nefertiti" is ready to jibe now but ours is almost complete. We have closed on her but not so close as the telephoto lense indicates.

"Constellation's" spinnaker hasn't broken once. We are only a length astern and gaining.

"Nefertiti's" superb crew finally muffs one in their haste to keep their wind clear. We have gained an overlap and are gaining fast.

There was little comment from the crew, mostly silence broken by someone, I don't remember who, saying almost inaudibly, "Good man, Eric." Then we broke up, soon arrived at the dock and scurried back to Castle Hill.

Before the evening was over, however, there wasn't a crew member who didn't seek me out alone, saying something the jist of which was, "You can do it, Reynard."

"Reynard" all of a sudden wasn't so sure, and for the first time all summer, I had trouble getting to sleep.

Next day the "Beat the Bird" pins and flags which we had made up as a part of our psychological warfare were out in force, and half the crew had the same message emblazoned with magic marker on some part of their anatomy. Charlotte eschewed this but gave me an extra good kiss as I left *Chaperone* to go aboard and said, "You can beat Bill, Bob," as though she really meant it.

Towing out, I tried to catnap below with no success at all and was glad when we reached the starting area, hoisted main and cast off. Eric sailed her around while we checked the line, decided on No. 2 5-ounce jib, got the most likely spinnakers in their pipe berth launching pads, and received the latest weather report from *Chaperone*. Sou'west 8–12, chance of fog, was the gist of it. *Eagle*'s main seemed very flat. They must be expecting it to come on. We were using our No. 1, the main we now considered our all-around sail. Good in light, good also in a breeze through flattening by our bending boom, the most successful of the innovations we tried.

Finally course signals were hoisted and Eric signaled me and said, "O.K., Bob, she's yours."

It felt good to have something to hold onto, something to do, and as I felt *Constellation*'s eager response I began to feel better.

By the time the 10-minute gun sounded, all butterflies had disappeared, or perhaps I was just too busy to notice them. Bill approached from windward of us where we were sailing to leeward of the line and at about its midpoint. Just as the warning gun sounded, they broke jib. Obviously he was out to get us early. We broke ours and the circling began. *Eagle* got a bit the better of it and started getting on our tail, so we headed for the Committee boat at the weather end and started

Both boats have jibed once more and are headed for the line two miles away on our leeward bow. Being to leeward we can't break clear but the line favors us and we win by 15 feet. Sweet revenge for our loss to "Nefertiti" in June.

circling it. At the 5-minute gun he had closed no further and I realized we would be able to do what we wanted. What we wanted was clear air and, since the leeward end was favored, we leaned toward being to leeward. I say "leaned" because we also felt that the first boat in toward the Pt. Jude shore would get headed and this made a windward start also attractive, despite its initial disadvantage. I decided we would go for whichever end seemed to assure us the best chance for free air. I felt *Constellation* might have a slight edge in speed, especially in view of *Eagle*'s flat main and the 8-knot wind then blowing.

Finally the decision was easy since there were just 2 minutes left when we completed a turn around the Committee boat, with *Eagle* still to complete hers. Since the line had been timed at over 2 minutes long, we could reach down it and be assured of being clear and with good speed. If we made one more circle, we would have trouble getting full headway and *Eagle* might maneuver to get a safe leeward on us.

"Trim for speed," I called as we headed for a point a bit over one length below the starting mark. With 10 seconds to go we trimmed down, sharpened up and shot across near the leeward end and going flat out. *Eagle* had fishtailed a bit to get well enough behind to avoid our backwind and at the gun she too was hard on the wind and traveling. It was a virtually even start but slightly in our favor due to being on the preferred end of the line. *Eagle* was well back on our quarter and there was no worry about our being blanketed. Instead, if we could squeeze up half a length, we just might backwind her.

I tried sailing a bit higher than one would for best speed, hoping *Eagle* would find it less to her liking to sail so high. For a couple of minutes Cox drove and footed us ever so slightly but in the process sagged off dangerously close to our backwind. To avoid this, he sharpened up and then the bearing started dropping perceptibly.

Five minutes after the start it was apparent we had improved our position and it suddenly dawned on me that my role had been to start us, with no mention of continuing to sail thereafter. "Come on, Eric," I called. "Your turn. I think you can squeeze her." "No, you keep her, Bob, you're doing fine," he replied. I didn't argue. "O.K., but sing out when you want to take her."

Slowly but steadily *Eagle* dropped back and down on us. Just as we were about to backwind her, she went about. We were ready, of course, waited half a length to be sure of being well clear of her backwind and then flipped over onto port tack with her.

"Eagle" and "Constellation" begin pre-start circling. It is July 17 and I'm making my first start.

"Eagle" has gained, is close to getting on our tail but we are still clear. Less than five minutes to go.

We eased both main and jib a few inches from the trim we had used while squeezing on starboard tack and gave *Constellation* her head. She soon was up to better than 8 knots. *Eagle* had eased even more and was sagging off to leeward. Dunny took bearings on the compass and confirmed an impression I had hardly dared believe—we were dropping her back on bearing as well as eating out to windward! We tried easing still more to see if speed would increase. It didn't, so we trimmed back. We were giving her a good rap full but *Eagle* seemed almost to be close-reaching, she was sagging off so. We could see adjustments being made to her outhaul and downhaul and Cox himself even left the wheel to supervise these alterations. Nothing seemed to work and we continued to work out and ahead.

When *Eagle* had to tack to clear the Pt. Jude shore, we crossed her by over 200 yards. In several ensuing tacks, we gained still more.

Then a mile from the mark we saw a wall of fog moving in on us. Thick. Dunny had just time to cut us in with a round of bearings and we were swallowed up. *Eagle* was lost to sight, as were all spectators. We were in Dunny's hands now. He figured calmly, ran the DR forward on his circular plotting board and suggested we tack for it in 5 minutes, 10 seconds. We tacked on cue, Eric took the wheel to be ready for our slide on the first reach, and all hands fell silent listening for the Pt. Jude bell. It seemed hours before Larry first heard it, apparently dead ahead. We leapt on and a minute later spotted the buoy not 50 yards ahead and 10 yards to leeward of our course. Score 4.0 for the navigator!

As we rounded, I recognized Corny Shields' Chris Craft hovering near the buoy. We sailed blind all that leg, seeing neither *Eagle* nor spectators. Dunny figured our time and Eric concentrated on the compass. With time up, we again heard a bell, this time pretty well to leeward. We held on for a minute, just to be sure, then jibed as the sound of the buoy dropped aft to our quarter. We had surely rounded it, though we never did see it. Just as surely, we would lose ground to *Eagle*, provided she hit it on the nose.

With an inexact point of departure, our problem of hitting the third mark, which was the starting buoy, was accentuated. It was, however, one of the inner torpedo range buoys and we hoped to spot one of the intermediate ones along our route. We knew we were to the east of them, since we had rounded the second mark wide, but how far to the east? Dunny set a course several degrees to the left of the base course

A minute to the start. "Constellation" goes for the leeward end. "Eagle" wipes off to avoid being early at the windward end.

Both boats cross as the starting smoke blows past. Despite what the telephoto lens seems to indicate "Constellation" is clear ahead but well to leeward and "Eagle" has clear air free of our backwind.

A few minutes later we have worked up, backwinded "Eagle" and forced her to tack. We follow suit. Though the race is cancelled by fog, with "Constellation" well ahead, the July trials end on a high note.

and while part of the crew concentrated on keeping *Constellation* moving, the remainder looked and listened. There never was a thicker fog. We could see no more than one length ahead. We could hear spectator boats all around us, and occasionally got a glimpse of one. We never did see the intermediate buoys, but we did hear each one as we passed it, and each one seemed a bit nearer.

Finally we had but one buoy to go. We didn't hear it until we were almost abeam, and had to alter course sharply to close it. Finally it loomed out of the fog and right beside it was the Committee boat with a "Race Off" signal flying. This was no weather to sail a second time around, but still we were disappointed at not having a chance to pin a loss on *Eagle*. Or would it have been a loss? We had lost ground at the second mark and there was a chance she had passed us. As we hovered around the Committee boat, however, and looked back up the course through the fog, *Eagle*'s blue top spinnaker suddenly loomed into sight. She was 2 minutes behind at that time and upon sight of her, cheers erupted from our crew. We hadn't won officially, but there was no doubt she had been saved by the fog alone.

Corny Shields later reported timing her as 4 minutes behind us at the weather mark. She had hit the next two on the nose, thanks to her Omni set, which we didn't have, but she was still well behind.

It was an exuberant post-mortem we held while towing in, and the crew seemed not to believe me when I pointed out that *Eagle's* flat main may have been the cause of her poor showing.

The shipyard hands and our wives were equally excited when we greeted each other at the dock. Soon there were reporters and crowds of well-wishers swarming down the pier. You would think we had just won the Cup instead of having a race called off.

We were elated to learn a short time later that there would be the same pairings next day, and there were many brave words spoken as to what we would do to the Bird. From the *Eagle* camp came equally brave pronouncements. They wanted to prove that this one "loss" was a fluke and that with another main they would rebound. The truth was that both camps were not at all sure what the real story was but both, with some trepidation, wanted to find out.

Alas, we were fated not to. There was more thick fog the next day and the Committee canceled the race before the start. And that was the end of the July trials.

They had ended on a high note for us, but upon reflection the next day we realized the enormity of the task still before us. Here it was July 19 and in fourteen races *Eagle* had yet to taste defeat. She had won all six races she sailed in the Observation trials, while our record was four wins and two losses (one through fouling the Committee boat, but still a loss). Still our one loss to *Eagle* had been a close one and our moral victory on the day of the fog, while not going into the record book, had surely made an impression on the Selection Committee. It had also left its mark on the crew of *American Eagle* and a more pleasant mark on our crew.

The trials had also demonstrated that, barring a complete reversal, the issue was now between *Eagle* and ourselves, with *Easterner*, *Columbia* and *Nefertiti* out of it. Ev Morris's July 19 article in the *New York Herald Tribune* was headlined "*Constellation* Threat to *Eagle.*" In a subsequent summing-up he wrote: "Unless some radical form reversals occur among the older boats, the fight for selection will be between the 1964 creations, *American Eagle* and *Constellation.*" He then continued, "The Bill Luders' designed *Eagle*, unbeaten in 14 races this summer although admittedly badly shaken in one which was canceled while in progress, is the boat the others have to catch." Truer words were never spoken, but still there wasn't a man on our boat, which had never beaten *Eagle,* who didn't feel we had a great chance to catch her. We had come a long way from those dark days of June 1.

Coming up was the New York Yacht Club Cruise, a fun interval of races which supposedly didn't count toward selection, yet ones which would serve to tell us whether we were living in a fool's paradise. We could hardly wait for the cruise to start, not knowing it would commence on a note of disaster to *Constellation* and to our hopes.

The New York Yacht Club Cruise

Disaster, Then Triumph

AT THE CONCLUSION of the Observation Trials, all hands had a couple of days off, our first in a month. This time we went home without our tails between our legs. Friends were ecstatic about our near win over *Eagle*, but all I could think was "one rose does not a summer make." Still we were showing steady improvement, and momentum, in any sport, is not to be discounted.

I spent two hectic days in *Yachting*'s office, accomplishing little more than to discover that while I was off living it up, the boys were minding the store real well.

Charlotte and I drove back to Castle Hill the afternoon of July 22 and next day went aboard one of the two cruise yachts Walter and Eric had chartered to house the crew during the cruise. We were going in style. As we entered New London that afternoon, we met the Portuguese full-rigged ship *Chagres*, under sail and heading east through Fisher's Island Sound, a bone in her teeth. A magnificent sight.

Another magnificent sight was the New York Yacht Club fleet at anchor in the Thames River, with *Constellation*, which Bill Burton and his crew had towed down earlier, looking like the Queen of the May even in that fine assemblage. She looked fast even at rest, but so did *Eagle*, *Nefertiti*, *Easterner* and the British Twelve *Norsaga*. *Columbia* was not going on the cruise. Twelves just can't look anything but fast. It suddenly felt very good to be back.

Next morning there was a steady drizzle driven by a 20–25-knot easterly. Great day for a race, and a chance to demonstrate whether *Constellation* could go with *American Eagle* in a knockdown drag out. It had been decided that I should start and that Eric and I would take turns steering thereafter. The course was a reach from Sarah's Ledge, past Race Rock to Cerberus buoy, and then a beat to Block Island. We chose the No. 2 main, not because we thought it was better under these conditions, but in the belief that here was an opportunity to evaluate it in a race which supposedly didn't count. It was, I feel, a bad decision because if we had shown poorly in a breeze because of it and never had another hard thrash later, the Selection Committee might conclude we were only a light-weather boat.

The line greatly favored the leeward end, and all five Twelves made for it. *Easterner* led the approach, *Nefertiti* second and us third, with me a bit worried that even we were pressing it. *Easterner* zigged and zagged to kill and *Nefertiti* luffed up, with us overlapping her to windward. This was putting us nearer the short end of the line, but when Hood bore off for it, I followed a length to windward, with our bow about 10 feet behind *Neffie's*. As the gun sounded, we could tell *Easterner* was early and hence were not too startled by the recall signal. But there were two blasts. Was it *Neffie* or us? We held on until Ted passed the word that they were calling our number. Despite being slightly behind him, the angle of the line put us early by a whisker.

It was 1 minute, 30 seconds before we had returned and started, several lengths behind *Easterner* and seemingly miles behind the others, all of which had made near-perfect starts. Best of all was *Norsaga's*. They had shot through a hole to leeward of *Nefertiti* when she luffed and couldn't have been more than a second late, right on the favored end.

In desperation and forgetting the maxim that "when behind, stay close and wait for a real opportunity," we set spinnaker. It made a great sight for the spectators, I am sure, but all it did for us was lay us over. The wind was just too far forward, and within minutes it was apparent we were losing. We doused it and reset jib, now even further behind. Thereafter on the reach to Cerberus we gained noticeably on *Easterner* and almost caught *Norsaga*, but just about held our own on *Eagle* and *Nefertiti*, which were well in front and hooked in a real battle.

Eric took the wheel just before reaching Cerberus, we rounded, started grinding in main and jib and even before they were fully sheeted home had shot right through *Norsaga's* lee. One down and four to go.

It was not to be. In the next instant there was a sharp snap aloft. The boom crashed down on the leeward coffee grinder, with Fred Kulicke

A sharp snap and seconds later our once proud mast looked like this. We were down but far from out.

hitting the deck beside the winch. He had reacted instinctively and thereby saved possible injury. I had reached to grab Fred and drag him back inboard if necessary and hence hadn't been able to look aloft. I didn't have to—it was apparent to all hands instantly that our tall, proud mast was gone.

When Fred started wriggling to windward, obviously unhurt, I looked aloft for the first time. The top third of our mast was dangling almost straight down, supported by a thread of aluminum and swinging in a wild arc. It had broken a couple of feet below the titanium section. We later found it was no fault of the mast but rather of a titanium clevis which was a sixteenth of an inch below the designed diameter. The metal was so strong that being this fraction undersize had reduced strength by 7,000 pounds, the tolerance of safety allowed for. The companion clevis on the other side, which was also undersize, when tested later in a laboratory broke at 15,000 pounds instead of the 22,000 it was supposed to stand. On an ocean racer, fittings have a 3 to 1 safety margin, but on Twelves, in the interest of saving weight and windage, 1½ to 1 is common practice. All well and good, but only if the fitting is manufactured exactly to the proper tolerance.

In the next hour, however, we were much too busy to think about the cause. Rod Stephens, who had joined our crew for the cruise when the crew limit was waived, was hoisted up the stump of the mast. With *Constellation* rolling badly despite our heading dead downwind toward Gull Island, he managed to lasso the wild-swinging top of the mast, lash it to the boat and then after unscrewing the masthead fitting, pull the main down, apparently undamaged. Rod is never happier than when aloft, faced with a challenge. Does anyone wear fifty-five years as well?

With things as well secured as we could make them, *Chaperone* threw us a towline and started us on a wild ride to Newport where our spare, all-aluminum mast awaited. Half the crew embarked on Briggs Cunningham's "5 Gs," were whisked in to New London, and then drove on to Newport to start preparations for a switch.

I stayed with the boat on what turned out to be the wettest tow of my life. *Chaperone* was a born towboat and slammed into the huge seas at 8 knots. We knifed through them, but in the process heavy water swept our decks almost continuously. Our hatches were not designed for ocean racing, and a steady stream of water cascaded below, soaking everything. It was cold on deck, just as cold below, but the inflow of water did give some compensation. We had to pump continuously, working in shifts, and this kept us warm. The influx of water also resulted in our putting canvas coverings over our hatches, a modification which served us well later on towing to the start on heavy weather days and also while racing.

At the moment, however, we could see nothing good in our predicament and instead possible disaster. Our titanium-topped spar was lost to us for an indefinite time and though we had a good aluminum spare there was no guarantee that it would prove as effective. Also the careful tuning which we had worked on for weeks might be hard to recapture. In 1962 *Columbia* never seemed quite the same after losing her mast.

We were, however, strangely optimistic. This was just one more challenge, and we were beginning to overcome so many others that we felt one more wouldn't break us.

As we towed in to Newport Shipyard late in the day, we could see the crane already in place, all key shipyard workers on hand and the other half of our crew standing by our spare mast which had already been removed from *Nereus* and placed adjacent to the crane.

Within a half hour our broken spar had been pulled free and shortly after dark the new one was in place. We attached shrouds and stays, without worrying about tuning, and by 10 o'clock were back at Castle Hill, wet, cold, tired but strangely elated. *Constellation* was again a sailboat, 30 miles away from and less than 12 hours after her disaster.

Next day a fierce nor'wester canceled the race from Block Island to Newport, and hence we missed nothing. As the fleet beat over under shortened sail, we were busy tuning *Constellation*. I say we, but in reality it was largely Rod Stephens and Don Wakeman. They were aloft practically all day. The rest of us busied ourselves getting all gear for the new mast in order. This included checking all the clevis pins for size and instituting a crash program of getting borderline ones replaced. We also washed and dried sails which had been soaked from our tow. It was almost dark when we were through. We felt a bit proud as the other Twelves sailed into the harbor in the afternoon and gave startled glances our way upon seeing us rigged and apparently ready.

We were on board early next morning for the race for the Caritas Cup for Twelves. There was an 8–10-knot sou'wester blowing as we towed out to the starting line. Rod was aloft all the way out, putting finishing touches to our tuning, and didn't come down until course signals had been hoisted and I had taken the wheel. The course was a 19-mile triangle, with a 7-mile beat to Pt. Jude buoy followed by a reach to the outer torpedo buoy and a spinnaker reach home. Our opponents were the same as two days before, with the exception of *Easterner*, which elected to go after the Queen's Cup (which she won by little over a minute from *Bolero*). Charlie Hovey had decided not to enter the final trials in his once-promising but now somewhat outclassed war horse and hence preferred in this one race to tackle the top ocean racers under the Cruising Club Rule.

The line favored the leeward end quite drastically, and I told myself not to be gun shy just because I had been over early and to go for it. I was a bit surprised to see only *Eagle* also going for that end and pleased to get across first at the favored end and with a safe leeward on *American Eagle*. We tacked to cover her shortly after she put about and crossed *Nefertiti* and *Norsaga* easily.

This time we didn't fly away from *Eagle* as we had in our previous meeting, but we did outpoint her and footed almost as fast. We were clearly leaving her, though it was close all the way in to the Pt. Jude shore. Cox was footing rather than pointing, partly because *Eagle*

"Constellation" in the lead, nearing the finish in her first victory over "American Eagle", two days after losing her mast. We were on our way at last.

couldn't seem to point with us and partly because he anticipated a header as he approached the shore. He got it, and our clear lead virtually evaporated. Still when she tacked we were able to cross by three lengths, tacked right on her and matched her tack for tack all the way to the mark, opening up steadily. I can still remember our crew's excited passing of the word "We're ahead of *Eagle*" when we first realized we could surely cross her.

We led by just over 1 minute at the mark. A good distance at the speed Twelves travel, but, knowing *Eagle's* reaching ability, I wished it had been twice as far. On the close reach she gained only slightly, rounding the second mark 58 seconds behind. Just 6 miles to go and we would have our first real win over our season-long tormentor.

I turned the wheel over to Eric for the spinnaker reach home. *Eagle's* spinnaker looked better and stadimeter readings soon showed she was gaining. She tried to suck us up by sailing high, but we didn't bite and held down almost for the finish. This race we wanted over as fast as possible. Still *Eagle* came, but as we passed a buoy midway between the last mark and the finish, it was apparent from the stadimeter that she had closed the distance by only one fourth after covering half the leg. At this rate we had her.

And have her we did, roaring across the finish line in a strengthening wind at 14:34:48, with *American Eagle* 29 seconds later and *Nefertiti* and *Norsaga* well back. I mention the precise time because this instance on July 26 was for us a historic moment—our first win over a previously invincible boat, and in as fair a breeze as you could hope to find. At the gun the entire crew leaped into the cockpit like the charge of the light brigade, screaming like banshees, slapping backs and shaking hands all around. We were on our way. Best of all, our replacement mast seemed fine, and further tuning would improve it. Twenty-nine seconds isn't much, but for that day it would serve. But could we do it again?

Not the next day! On the 26-mile run from Newport to Padanarum in a fresh sou'wester, I lost the race right at the start by being over early again. I've always felt that any good starter is apt to be over early once a summer—otherwise he isn't getting close enough. But over twice in three starts is poor, no matter how you slice it. I simply hadn't taken into account the fast rate at which a Twelve closes the line and in my desire to have full headway and not be late, had been pressing it.

This, however, turned out to be an encouraging race. On the reach to the Buzzards we passed *Norsaga* and *Easterner* and closed on *Nefertiti* and *Eagle*. On the run down the bay we passed *Nefertiti* and began to give *American Eagle* fits before losing to her by 41 seconds. This was less than we had spotted her at the start, and we had been hampered by having to sail through the intervening boats. After our poor reaching performance of the day before, we were greatly heartened. We had used a different Hood spinnaker and it had made quite a difference.

The next two races proved that our optimism was well founded. The race to Edgartown was canceled due to fog, but on July 30 we won the 21-mile run from Edgartown to Nantucket in light air. *Eagle* was just 28 seconds behind us, but behind she was. Eric started and was conservative. Hence we were third at the first mark. Then we took off, passed *Nefertiti* and went by *Eagle* about 5 miles from the finish.

The following race, from Nantucket to Woods Hole, Eric started again, directly in *Eagle*'s backwind, and well behind *Nefertiti*, which took us all. He then turned the wheel over to me for the long and short leg beat to the first buoy. We squeezed out of *Eagle*'s backwind, dropping back in the process, but then proceeded to fly. At the mark it was *Neffie* first by a whisker, *Constellation* second and *Eagle* three lengths astern. On the ensuing reach, positions were unchanged and then we squared away on a spinnaker reach. We soon got by *Nefertiti* and match-raced *Eagle* all the way to the finish. The wind was spotty. At times *Eagle* drew within one length of us, at others we opened up to 500 yards, only to have her close up when we ran into a hole. With 3 miles to go, she closed to one length when the northerly dropped entirely. But that's as far as she went. We got the new sou'wester a few seconds earlier than she and coasted home to win by 1 minute, 6 seconds.

The next day, last of the cruise, proved to us to be the most exciting. I was again elected to start and distinguished myself on only two counts: 1, I wasn't over early, and 2, we were ahead of *Eagle*. All the other Twelves led us across.

But in the 5–6-knot air it wasn't long before the two last were leading the pack. *Eagle* tacked first to the west and we followed shortly on her weather quarter. For a while we were leading, then *Eagle* got the header she was looking for and we seemed about even. Hard to tell. Finally she tacked and we could see her bearing dropping back ever so slightly. We tacked on her lee bow for a safe leeward less than a length clear ahead. The safe leeward was just beginning to make itself

Fleet racing on the New York Yacht Club Cruise from Newport to Padanaram. "Eagle" (foreground) reached by "Nefertiti" to win. "Constellation" closed fast after a premature start to take second. "Eagle's" small spinnaker proved superior to "Neffie's" much larger one.

felt when all of a sudden our 3-ounce hankless jib came tumbling down and fell into the water. We had a 5-ounce jib hanked on and hoisted in just over a minute, but by then the damage was done. *Eagle* was on our wind, and with the 5-ounce we didn't have the same zip. Cause of the failure was a too light jib luff wire, considering the tremendous tension we put on it—about 3 tons. We later replaced all our hankless jib luffs with larger diameter wire.

But at the moment we were less interested in the cause than the effect. *Eagle* was murdering us. She was on our wind, she was feeding into better air and she flew away as she had in June.

When we rounded the weather mark 450 yards behind, with a spinnaker run and spinnaker reach to go, we had little hope. Eric took the wheel and I took stadimeter readings to verify what my eyes were telling me. We were closing fast. On the previous leg *Eagle* had been feeding into stronger wind. Now we were bringing up a better breeze with our small 45 spinnaker bulging.

The gang on *Eagle* misconstrued the reason and shifted to a different chute, one which we were happy to note didn't look as well. Finally the breeze filled in evenly and our rate of gain slowed. But we still kept closing and were just 100 yards behind as we jibed and started the 5-mile reach for the finish. On the closer reach our spinnaker looked considerably better than *Eagle's*, and we closed steadily. Two thirds of the way we were only half a length behind, and Bill Cox must have developed a real crick in his neck looking back at us every few seconds. With less than half a mile to go, we became overlapped. *Eagle* luffed us slowly, but there was no stopping *Constellation*. Just 300 yards from the finish, we swept by and *Eagle*, demoralized by then, made a couple of sloppy jibes and we were home free, winning a race which had seemed lost, by 28 seconds.

More important, we had won the last three in a row and four out of six starts on the Cruise. Every win over *American Eagle* had been a real nail-nibbler, but now we were beginning to win the close ones instead of losing them. While the New York Yacht Club Cruise results didn't count toward selection, they gave us a much-needed lift and couldn't help but worry the *American Eagle* crew. Since they were working hard already, worry couldn't spur them to higher effort. It could only cause, we hoped, a tightening up on their part in which desperation might take the place of good judgment. When we were losing in June and early July, we had the advantage of knowing that there was lots of time to correct errors and to sharpen up. Hence our losses were in some respects an advantage. Losses in the last races before the final trials, however, could only have a demoralizing effect on *Eagle*, since they had been expending full effort throughout.

We had, of course, been very closely pressed in each one of our wins, and we had lost two of the six. Our four wins still put us way behind *Eagle* for the year, and we realized we still had a long way to go to beat her. For the first time since the very first race, however, we had confidence—not blind confidence which we had then, but instead a belief in our boat and in ourselves based on some tangible victories. We knew the road ahead would be rough, we knew we could very easily lose to *American Eagle*, but we also felt for the first time in two months that the tide had turned slightly in our favor. This degree of confidence only served to loosen us, to enable us to think straight and sail well without undue tension, without lulling us into any complacency. We resolved to prepare for the final trials harder than ever, but because we knew we had a solid chance the prospect of this effort was a pleasant one. We were perhaps more determined than we had been all summer, but not grimly so. If it's possible for a crew in contention to be loose prior to the final trials, we were that crew, but, believe me, only in relative terms.

There was only one unpleasantness at this time and that was of our own making. Eric and I and those who were advising us all felt that we could use a truly experienced hand in the cockpit. It had been decided that from here on out I would start each race and do most of the steering thereafter, though Eric would remain as skipper. It's a great help to have a tactician on board in which one has great confidence, someone to act as a second pair of eyes and with whom the strategy of the race can be discussed as it progresses. Of course we had Eric and Dunny, both well qualified for this role, but it was the consensus that it would help to have additional experience.

Rod Stephens had sailed with us throughout the cruise, and his contribution then was immense. He had the confidence of the entire crew from the foredeck back to the wheel, and he had served as a catalyst to bring us all together as a more efficient team. He has been referred to as "The Great God Rod," and in a nice way that's the way we felt about him. We all knew of his experience on *Dorade* in winning the Trans-Atlantic Race at age twenty-two, and his successful America's Cup campaigns on *Ranger* and *Columbia*. We concluded quite easily that we would be a better boat with Rod aboard.

There was one other we considered for this role—Jerry Driscoll from California. Jerry had been of great help to me when I was starting *Nereus* against *Constellation*. He was a crack sailor, as witness his Star Class World Championship, and he was an equally good seaman. He also had the advantage of being in his forties—Rod was fifty-five, though I still find it hard to believe. We finally decided in favor of Rod, partly because of his real help on the Cruise, partly because he could do everything on board so well and especially because I couldn't think of anyone I would rather have sailing with me.

So, what's so unpleasant about having Rod come on board? Simply that to add Rod it meant dropping someone from our regular crew that had worked so long and so effectively. The real rub was that there was no weak member on board, no one we didn't want to keep.

Eric felt, with considerable logic, that since Rod was being added largely to increase the cockpit talent, the opening must be found in the afterguard, and that meant dropping our navigator, Dun Gifford. Both Rod and I were in favor of dropping someone from the deck gang, partly because Rod could pinch-hit there superlatively, partly because we felt Dunny could also move out of the cockpit when not navigating, but most of all because there was no more popular guy on board and we wanted to retain the efficiency which comes from a happy ship. Eric argued, however, that personal considerations should not enter the decision, contended that Rod could do the navigation with ease (Agreed) and that it would be less disruptive to make a single swap involving only the cockpit rather than having Rod join the cockpit and Dunny replace someone on deck while not navigating.

There was, of course, much to be said on both sides, and Eric might well have been right. Subsequent results seemed to have borne him out, but still it was a decision which both Rod and I opposed to the end. We got rid of as fine a 12-Meter navigator and as fine a guy as I know. I hope he takes some solace in being known as "Alternate to Rod Stephens." It's sort of like saying alternate to Babe Ruth or Mickey Mantle.

Dunny took it hard, but he stuck with us, worked as hard as ever on our trial spins, and how glad we all were, Rod in particular, to have him back on board for the third Cup Race against *Sovereign*.

But now I'm getting ahead of my story. Let's go back to those final two weeks before the final trials, weeks in which *Constellation* was brought to the peak of perfection, weeks in which we first saw the British under sail. They started by all hands heading home for a three-day breather, which enabled Charlotte and me to drive home, pick up our children, Rob, 16; Louise, 13; Anne, 6; and John, 3; and then bring them all up to Newport to remain until we were selected or eliminated. We were getting down to the wire and, win or lose, we wanted them to be a part of it. Rob and Louise enjoyed it fully, Anne and John enjoyed getting away from sitters and back with us, and Charlotte and I will remember August 1964 as the most trying yet most exciting and rewarding month of our lives, at least until September 1964 rolled around.

Sovereign and *Kurrewa V*

WHILE WE WERE OFF on the cruise, Newport was invaded by the redcoats and the green shirts—a band of big, burly, serious but captivating Englishmen—the crews of royal blue *Sovereign* and pea-green *Kurrewa V*.

Peter Scott, skipper of *Sovereign*, had arrived during the July trials. I had known Peter for ten years and quickly invited him and *Sovereign*'s designer, David Boyd, on board. We were glad to, partly because we felt it was by then too late for them to modify *Sovereign*, but also because we felt that the America's Cup competition, deadly serious though it is and must be, can be taken too seriously off the race course. We simply wanted them to see the boat we were so proud of.

David Boyd was especially interested in our fittings, and in particular our bendy boom. He avowed he considered it completely legal and only wished he had thought of it himself. We answered all their questions completely and without restraint. The America's Cup competition was suddenly becoming great fun.

I also enjoyed Peter Scott's obviously sincere belief that *Constellation* would be selected over *American Eagle* and the others. He said this, mind you, before we had beaten *Eagle* a single time, though after the "fog race" which had been canceled after we were leading. Peter had seen both *Eagle* and *Constellation* hauled out and as far as I could tell, his opinion was based on an impression that *Constellation*'s design had more potential. He expressed confidence that we would eventually sail her up to this potential and that, though close throughout, we would end up on top. Knowing Peter as I did, I realized he meant what he said. I only hoped he was right.

After we returned to Newport from the Cruise, Peter invited us aboard *Sovereign*. We had already seen her sailing, and in the smooth waters of Narragansett Bay she was as handsome a Twelve as you could hope to see—graceful, powerful and purposeful. Close scrutiny did nothing to spoil the image as regards the hull. She reminded me more of *American Eagle* than *Constellation*, with more beam, more flare than we had. Her wetted surface seemed similar to *Eagle's* too, but she had a considerably larger rudder, more in the 1962 style—all in all, a truly fine-looking hull.

Her deck and cockpit layout, however, were less impressive. There seemed to be many more cleats and fittings and she looked complicated. This was partly because she was different from *Constellation*, which was now so familiar to us. Still I found myself thankful we didn't have to handle *Sovereign's* gear.

Her main coffee grinders were linked and looked good. They were, however, linked by gears above deck—a small difference, perhaps, but it meant the weight was just that much higher. Her shrouds, spreaders, masthead fittings, stays, turnbuckles, and the like, seemed heavy and cumbersome compared to ours. Well made and serviceable, but more like something you would expect on an ocean racer than a Twelve. Good stuff but lacking in refinement and sure to cause more windage as well as weighing more.

Down below she was well laid out but again there seemed insufficient effort to save every ounce of weight the rule allowed.

In days ahead we saw her sails and were everlastingly grateful we were using ours instead. She didn't lack for numbers of them—in fact, she had far more sails than we did, but with the exception of one reaching spinnaker we were not ready to trade for any of them. We kept wondering, however, if they didn't have a few other sails we hadn't seen which they were keeping under wraps.

A few days later Owen Aisher, the driving force behind *Kurrewa V*, and Stugg Perry, her skipper, invited us aboard their pride and joy. There was, of course, great similarity to *Sovereign*, since both boats had the same hull. I can never understand why the British built two virtually identical boats when they have several capable designers. It seemed so much more likely to score a real advance if they gave themselves two chances by going to different designers or at least commissioning Boyd to come up with a different design. I believe their thinking was that since *Sovereign* had shown very well in the tank, their best bet was to stick with one hull design and let two different groups thus be able to refine their tuning, their arrangement of fittings and their

"Kurrewa V" and "Sovereign" (leading) had a number of close races off Newport but the dark blue boat usually came out on top. Her striped spinnaker was a beauty. Why was it usually in the bag? Perhaps too many sails to know which were the best.

sailing techniques. The spreader arrangement on the two boats was quite different but seemed equally crude (by American standards) on both.

Kurrewa V used a different jibing system, employing two poles. It appeared to work well, but this necessitated two poles continually on deck. Our spare pole (and *Sovereign*'s, too) was stored below, thus eliminating windage and getting its weight lower. The British just didn't seem to share our concern for weight reduction. They were keen sailors and highly intelligent men, but appeared to have the attitude, "What difference will a few pounds up high make in a boat weighing 30 tons?" If there was only one instance in which they had failed to save a few pounds of high weight, it would be insignificant. But by having an attitude that even a few ounces were important and by applying this attitude throughout, we managed very significant reductions in both weight and windage.

We came away from our pleasant tours of *Sovereign* and *Kurrewa* with the feeling that as far as fittings, rig and sails were concerned we had a real edge. About the hull, I didn't feel qualified to give an intelligent observation. The British hulls looked good, though we would not have traded for *Constellation*. If their hulls were superior, we felt this could overcome what we considered to be relatively clumsy rigs. Of course, our concern at that time was not at all with *Sovereign* or *Kurrewa*, but rather with a certain American boat which we had yet to beat in an official trial race.

When the British arrived in America, there were very few either in England or America who were not picking *Kurrewa* as the logical challenger. In their trials in England they were virtually even up—ten wins for *Kurrewa V*, nine for *Sovereign*. *Kurrewa V* however, had the better record upwind, was a newer boat and most observers felt that with more training she would equal *Sovereign*'s downwind ability. Owen Aisher's reputation as an organizer was renowned, and Stugg Perry, an Olympic Medalist, had more recent experience than Peter Scott and was deemed the more able big-boat helmsman. Peter's greatest success had been in dinghies and planing boats.

I'm rather proud of myself, in the face of this weight of logic, to have been a virtual voice in the wilderness in picking *Sovereign*. I did it solely on the basis of my respect for Peter. He has a habit of excelling in everything he does, and this I felt was something he would rather excel in than anything else. I had noted, also, that Peter had skippered only half of the earlier races, but that his record in the races he sailed had been much the best. Now that he had been named skipper officially, I felt *Sovereign* would come alive.

Indicative of his thoroughness was a notebook he kept in which he sketched the progress of every race sailed. Most important was a list of lessons learned. All good sailors make mistakes. The very good ones

"Sovereign's" able crew. They deserved a better horse. (Left to right in front) Peter Scott, Bert Shaw, Richard Haseldon, John Scaife, John Scott, Paul Anderson, Don Bradby and Roger Fuger. (In back) Anthony Boyden, Eric Maxwell, Jim McLean, Bobby Bruce, Geoff Merritt, Robert Dean, Dick Page and David Marques.

always recognize the mistakes as being just that. They don't alibi for them—they learn from them. Peter's book, which he took pleasure in showing me, was a fascinating document. I've always kept a mental book. Yacht races are the one thing in life I seem to be able to remember in detail. But after glancing at Peter's notebook, I began to wonder if I were not remiss in failing to keep better records. I decided not to try—everyone has to do things in his own way. But for his particular way, Peter's book was a classic.

I don't think my opinion that *Sovereign* would win was colored by the fact that I quite frankly hoped she would. This preference was no reflection on Aisher or Perry, two of the very finest guys you could hope to know. I simply wanted Peter Scott to win because we had been friends for many years, and the prospect of doing battle for the America's Cup with a friend (if we could both just hurdle the big obstacles still ahead of us) added just one more fillip to a lifelong dream. I hope Stugg never felt I was rooting against him. I wasn't really, but I *was* rooting for Peter.

The first set of British trials started on August 9. Since we were out sailing anyway, we just happened to do our drill in the area of their race. We felt both boats missed opportunities to clobber each other at the start. Eventually they got away roughly even, both with clear air. To my surprise, *Sovereign* pointed higher, footed well and was in the driver's seat at the first mark. Downwind *Kurrewa V* came on like gangbusters, largely because of a better-looking spinnaker. Again *Sovereign* went ahead upwind and proceeded to win in convincing style. Both boats seemed well sailed. *Sovereign's* sails looked fairly good and noticeably better than *Kurrewa's*.

We only watched one other race in their preliminary trials, again won by *Sovereign*. This was a thriller, with the lead changing hands several times and *Sovereign* going ahead to stay by getting an overlap at the final leeward mark, driving *Kurrewa V* wide of the mark and jibing eventually right on top of her. It was a pretty piece of work.

On the last beat we sailed along for a few minutes about a quarter mile on their leeward beam. Our bearing stayed roughly the same, but we seemed to be squeezing up under them at a most satisfying rate. "Must be a different wind down here," I said. Subsequent events proved me wrong. I just couldn't believe then that we could point that much higher.

We peeled off before anything conclusive could be learned, but we had seen just enough to gain the impression we could handle them if we ever got the chance. That was the big question. Could we beat *Eagle* and the other American boats? In a couple of weeks we would start finding out. In the meantime there was much to be done.

The first set of British trials ended in *Sovereign's* favor. *Kurrewa V* had work to do, too, and *Sovereign's* margins had been so slight that Peter and his crew could hardly start counting their chickens. Hence the next few days saw four American Twelves and two British sailing from early morning to dusk, practicing, looking at sails, trying new sails. There suddenly was so little time!

Perfecting *Constellation*

W HILE IT WOULD HAVE BEEN FUN to watch more of the British trials and perhaps instructive, too, we just didn't have time. There were more immediate fish to fry.

Our handling on the Cruise had been basically sharp, but we were still slow on changing from one hanked jib to another. The procedure was to first set a hankless interim jib, the size of a working jib. Next, the jib which was hanked on (say a 5-ounce) was lowered and unhanked. Next the replacement jib (in this instance a 9-ounce) was hanked on and hoisted and when broken out and trimmed, the interim jib was lowered and cleared away. By using this method a headsail was always up and drawing. With the interim jib on, speed remained the same but we were unable to point as high (about 8° lower).

We were taking between 4 and 5 minutes to complete the evolution from the first call, with the crew lying down, nothing rigged beforehand and the interim and replacement jibs below, until the interim jib and replaced jib were back down below. In that time we lost about one length and a half. We figured, therefore, if we could get below 3 minutes we could nearly half the loss.

We tried it several times a day, always under stop watch. At first progress was slow, but eventually we did get under 3 minutes. It was a sight of ordered confusion to see the crew spring to their feet and scurry about. Our timing improvement came from each man ultimately knowing instinctively just what to do at each stage of the evolution, with no lost motion, no duplication of effort and with no one getting in the other fellow's way.

I will dream for the rest of my life, and dream in vain, of sailing on an ocean racer with such a coordinated crew.

We also practiced changing spinnakers, setting the second one inside the one already up, and then dousing the original sail. We got it down so pat that there was never a break in the spinnaker and no discernible loss of speed or distance. This we were to use in races, but we never had a chance to show off our interim jib change. If you think I'm boasting, you are right. But only for our great crew and for Rod Stephens, who more than anyone else perfected these evolutions.

Of course we practiced jibes until we were limp. Finally a flubbed jibe was one in which the spinnaker partially collapsed for a bare instant. Almost always it remained hard full throughout.

I would have liked to practice starts, but unfortunately our broken mast was not yet repaired and hence *Nereus* was out of commission. We did try a few abortive efforts against Fenny Johnson's 67-foot ocean racer *Challenge*. She was a great boat, but *Constellation* turned sharper, accelerated faster and had a higher maximum speed. Glit Shields sailed her against me, but even when Glit got what would have been a controlling position in a Twelve (and he did so not infrequently), *Constellation*'s superiority let us wriggle off the hook. After one day, therefore, we called it off, feeling it might spoil our timing and give us false illusions of being great starters.

All of our various practice was important, but nothing quite so important as the work we did on our sails. The only new sails we bought were a second 3-ounce jib as a backstop to our present one, and an experimental spinnaker. We didn't like the new jib quite as much as the original, but were glad to have it in case the one we had let go. We had concluded that the 3-ounce was a better sail to set under all conditions than the 2.2-ounce. In 2 knots of breeze, the 2.2 was very slightly better, but it had less range, and from 3 knots to 6, the 3-ounce was far better. In less than 2 knots, our ¾-ounce "wind finder" was the answer. Therefore in the final trials we left the 2.2 ashore, in the interest of simplicity and also in order to improve our chances of having the right sail up in a variable breeze.

The new spinnaker was most interesting. It was made of Mylar, cross-hatched with Dacron threads to stop it from ripping. It was developed by Wally Ross, was lighter than our ¾-ounce nylon chutes yet had virtually no stretch, certainly less than our 1.5-ounce sails. We had high hopes for it, particularly for very light air and for reaching in any breeze. On its test sail we went well up Narragansett Bay, out of sight of Eagle and other prying eyes. It was blowing 25 knots, but we set it anyway, figuring then was the time to discover what it would

Fair weather or foul, we practiced every day. Here word has just come from the cockpit to set spinnaker.

Precise timing was essential on a jibe. If the helmsman bore off either too slowly or too fast it could spoil everything. When timed right the spinnaker never broke and jibing became as routine as tacking.

stand. It held! And it looked good. It was strange to have a sail you could look right through, but the Dacron threads which were designed to stop rips from spreading also made it easier to detect when it was collapsing. We decided to try it in the final trials, and packed it away, feeling rather smug. For secrecy's sake we listed it on our sail board as XL 50.

Imagine our disappointment to come sailing by a point of land a couple of days later and see *Eagle* flying a transparent chute!

As it turned out, *Eagle*'s was a flop the one time she raced with it. We raced with ours against *Columbia* on two legs. On one we flew, on the other we lost and we never tried it again, feeling that when the chips were down we wanted only sails whose capabilities we knew from long experience. This sail of Wally's, however, was a good one, and I suspect that the material, if used on a sail cut specifically for reaching, might well be a real winner.

Our other sails, two mains, two 5-ounce jibs, two 9-ounce jibs and 8 spinnakers, were all good, yet all received what was probably the most protracted recutting in the history of sailing. Our No. 1 main, which we were already referring to as our "winning main," had the least done to it—a bit of easing of the leech and some work to remove a few wrinkles aloft. After recutting, it looked just about the same (thank God!), but a shade better.

Our No. 2 main was a bit fuller, but we went so well in light air with our No. 1 that we figured we would never use the No. 2. We knew that in 10 knots and over the No. 1 was better, and we were not sure that the No. 2 was really better in lighter air. We mentioned to Ted Hood that what we really wished we had was a flat sail for wind speeds of 22 to 30 knots. From drifting conditions up to 22 knots we had great confidence in our No. 1—confidence based largely on our bendy boom, which made this wide range of effectiveness possible.

Upon hearing our reasoning, Ted Hood, Lee Van Gemert and Joe Pierce the Australian (look out in '67), who were Ted's right-hand men, all said it was no problem—just recut our light weather main into a real flat sail for extreme heavy weather. I couldn't believe it, but two days later our light weather main was back, looking like a totally different sail.

The spinnakers were looked at by Ted, Joe and Lee both from on board and from off the boat. We told them which ones we had found

Main cabin looking aft, two bunks and navigating nook to starboard. The port side had a bunk aft but was mostly sail bins for the genoas.

Buddy checks a spinnaker in its special pipe berth. Sails were flaked down into these "berths" and hoisted directly from them through the center hatch. Note chute behind Buddy to facilitate transport of jibs to forward hatch.

most effective in which wind strengths. The sailmakers would make notes and draw crude sketches of what they saw, would take them all ashore and a day or so later all would be back for another look. Some were recut two or three times, and each time they looked a trifle better for it.

The most protracted recutting was given to our jibs, easing a leech here, taking it up there, changing draft slightly. Some were recut five times before Joe was satisfied. Since Ted Hood was busy getting *Nefertiti* ready, Joe Pierce spent the most time with us. He was tireless and seemed never satisfied, even with sails which looked virtually perfect to us. We were careful to make only tentative suggestions of our own. Instead we put our complete confidence in Joe. If he wanted recutting, it was done, and done along his lines. He was fun to have on board and made a seemingly tedious job interesting. The Australians will not suffer for lack of good sails in 1967. Of that you can be sure.

Dunny had a fine navigating area to work from. He worked fast, however, and was almost always on deck.

While we were recutting, we saw *Eagle* trying new sails. It made us worry a bit that they might come up with something great, and what we saw of their sails looked good. Many of them were Hood sails. We asked Ted if we needed any more and he said no—better to perfect something already tested than to try to start from scratch. That suited us fine, because by now we knew our sails' capabilities for each strength of wind and were assured that the recutting would not (except in the case of our No. 2 main) change their basic characteristics but would, hopefully, improve them further in the same wind ranges they had gone well in before. The sails we had might seem like a lot, but by America's Cup standards, and compared to *American Eagle*, they were very few. As a result, we almost always set the right one, something *Eagle* often missed doing, to her great regret.

A few days before the final trials, repairs to our titanium-topped spar were completed. We debated resetting it but decided against it on the basis that the aluminum one was very finely tuned, we had gone very well with it, and why change a winning combination?

Throughout the final days, Rod Stephens was busy doing a myriad of little things—relocating the winch handle holders a few inches, adding a self-bailing trough in the fore part of our forward hatch, designing a zipper closure to cover this hatch, compensating the compasses till they were free of all error, tuning by the hour, checking each clevis, tang and other fitting for signs of wear and replacing with new parts which had been checked exhaustively. (We were not going to break any more masts.) A new chute in the forepeak was installed to speed getting headsails on deck. In making these and countless other modifications we thought always of weight. To save weight, we removed a few superfluous items. We discarded the direction finder, figuring DR was more reliable on a 4½-mile leg. The spare parts and tools were checked over carefully. The essential ones remained on board, but many were removed. A few days before the final trials we were measured in a light condition and found to our delight that we had gained no weight and could keep all our ballast. Then we were hauled and our entire crew joined the great gang at Newport Shipyard polishing our bottom till it shone. A new nonskid surface was applied to the deck, brightwork was revarnished, winches given a final servicing. We looked like a yacht, and an efficient one.

I hope the detailed description of our preparation hasn't been too

←
Every fitting, every bit of rigging was checked over for flaws, greased, oiled and in general made perfect.

tedious. I included it because it taught me, as never before, the importance of painstaking preparation if one hopes to win in fast company. It's a lesson I hope to remember on my own smaller boats, though I'll never practice it to quite the degree we did on *Constellation* except for the most major series. Doing so all the time would make racing too much work. But watch out for the guy who is willing to! Fanatical attention to many little details will help him beat you. But one lesson I hope to apply. Get your sailmaker to look at your sails as often as you can drag the poor soul away from his loft or his family. Then recut and recut again.

On August 16 we were eased back in the water, remeasured with all our gear and nineteen sails (more than we would ever carry) on board. We were exactly on our marks. Mentally we were on our marks too, ready and set to go. At least we would never be more ready. We knew the gang on *Eagle* had been working as hard as we, but since we could think of nothing more to do, we were strangely relaxed. Months of preparation had come to a climax. I felt we had reached our peak, rated our chances a bit better than fifty-fifty, and looked forward to the do-or-die battle that was to begin. After all, I loved sailing and this was the most exciting sailing I had ever embarked on, so why not enjoy it?

Charlotte was surprised when I fell asleep a few minutes after I turned in early the night before the final trials. I slept the night through, but not without dreams—disjointed dreams about sailing against a white sloop. Sometimes her skipper was identifiable as Bill Cox, sometimes we were behind, sometimes ahead, but before a race was finished, John Handel was beating on our door and hollering, "seven o'clock—all out for the America's Cup."

→
The greatest amount of time was spent in perfecting our sails and tuning. Here is the end result. Pure perfection. No hard spots, no tight or soft leeches, perfect slot between genoa and main. Note the bendy boom, our best single feature. Sight the mast. It is absolutely straight.

The Final Trials Begin

I DIDN'T FEEL QUITE SO CALM the next morning, Monday, August 17—date of the first race of the Final Trials. The mere name of this series was enough to excite anyone. A few straight losses and it could be curtains for us, and I found myself remembering the fact that *Eagle* had beaten us seven straight times early in the season and that *Nefertiti* and *Columbia* had both licked us. I knew we were better now, but still it was disquieting to realize that we were now at the do-or-die stage.

Our so-called Executive Committee, composed of Olin Stephens, Eric Ridder and Walter Gubelmann, had decided that henceforth I would not only start each race but would continue to steer as long as I desired. Eric was to retain the title of skipper, but it was made quite clear to me that while steering I would be largely responsible for where we went, not only for trying to make her go fast. This suited me fine, but don't think it wasn't sobering! Of course I would lean heavily on Rod and Eric. We acted as a triumvirate, and a most compatible one, since we almost invariably agreed.

I was pleased that our first selection race was against *Columbia*. We knew we were faster, knew we had a sharper crew, and I hoped we could outmaneuver her. And because I had so little experience at the wheel, I welcomed having an easier test first.

There was a 9-knot wind at the start, a start which found us crossing with a full head of steam 31 seconds ahead and to weather. From this vantage point, *Constellation* took over, outpointing and outfooting her older rival. With a lead of 3:45 at the first mark, it seemed a good time to try our Mylar spinnaker. We gained on one reach, lost on another. It was an inconclusive test, but sufficient to convince us that the sail was no breakthrough. Since we wanted nothing which wasn't tried and true at this stage, we put it back in the locker for good.

94

The number one enemy (all good friends)—brain trust of "American Eagle": Bill Stetson, tactician and alternate helmsman; Halsey Herreshoff, navigator; Bill Cox, skipper and Pete Du Pont syndicate organizer.

Eric sailed the latter part of this race, and we won easily by just over 5 minutes. The margin was not so important as the fact that we had never looked like a loser and everything had gone like clockwork. It was just the tonic we needed, because the following day we were paired with *American Eagle*. She had a pretty good tonic too, having taken *Nefertiti* in the first race by nearly 6 minutes.

Next day I was surprised to find myself strangely calm as the time for our crucial meeting with *American Eagle* approached. I have since wondered why and have concluded the explanation lay in the fact that I felt we had a slightly better boat, an excellent crew, and that we were as prepared as it was possible to be. I could think of nothing we would like to do if we had an extra week, except for start practice. We were like a prize fighter who has reached his peak in training the day before the fight and knows that further training would only make him stale. I didn't feel the least bit complacent, realized that we could very easily lose, but since we had done all we could, I did feel fatalistic. I also looked forward to the battle as something to be enjoyed.

Since we thought we were faster, our strategy called for getting clear air at the start, rather than the more risky tactic of trying to clobber the opposition (with a resulting good chance of being clobbered ourselves instead). By maneuvering between the ends of the line and well to leeward of it, the chances of getting blocked were minimal. Knowledge of this also helped reduce pressure and it was with keen anticipation

The august, experienced selection committee, faced with the thankless task of choosing one boat out of four final contenders—Henry Sears, Julian K. Roosevelt, Henry S. Morgan (chairman), Percy Chubb II, George R. Hinman, De Coursey Fales, W. Mahlon Dickerson. Even the losers felt they did a great job.

Sir Gordon Smith (white cap) was the British observer. The others are the great America's Cup Race Committee. (Left to right) Robert H. Wessmann, Willis M. Fanning, E. Jared Bliss, Jr., J. Burr Bartram, Jr., F. Briggs Dalzell (chairman), William Burnham.

that I approached the first showdown race. If, in trying to express my feelings, I've implied that I was as cool as the proverbial cucumber, I didn't mean it. I was keyed up, excited, somewhat nervous but at the same time eager rather than tense.

There was only a 6-knot wind blowing at the start. Circling began nearly 10 minutes before our start and, much to my delight, we managed to get on *Eagle*'s tail. Cox took refuge by circling the Committee boat, but as he started the fourth circle, we broke it off and went for a start on her lee bow as she completed the fourth circle. It worked O.K., with both boats approximately even, both with clear air and *Constellation* one length to leeward.

In five minutes we had squeezed up to force her about, tacked with her one length later and then just as we were losing a bit of our edge due to a header, a most delicious accident happened—to *Eagle*. Her hankless 3-ounce jib luff wire broke and the whole sail tumbled down, just as ours had in the last race of the Cruise. We watched with ill-concealed but quiet glee as they rushed below, hanked on a 5-ounce jib, hoisted it, broke it out and found that one of the hanks was twisted. They had to lower again. I watched Bill Cox bearing off in an effort to keep speed on under main alone, and I felt sorry for him. I felt glad for us, though, because at this stage of the summer there was no substitute for victory.

We were dead on their wind before they got everything squared away. Meanwhile the wind had been heading and I was surprised to hear Rod say, "You can fetch, Bob." Only 11 minutes had elapsed since the start, 6 minutes on this tack and it seemed hardly possible. The mark was invisible, but I knew Rod had kept a careful plot. "Are you sure, Rod?" I asked, not really doubting him, but wanting to be positive before tacking off *Eagle*'s wind. "I'm sure," he replied.

We tacked immediately thereafter and it was a joy to watch the stunned expression on the faces of *Eagle*'s crew. All hands had been so busy changing jibs that there was little time to consider the effect of the header. I saw Halsey Herreshoff dash below, emerge a half minute later and after a brief consultation with Bill Cox, they tacked on our weather quarter.

We fetched on the nose, thus gaining 100 yards by tacking on time instead of overstanding, as *Eagle* had. This was just one of the more graphic examples of the help Rod Stephens was to us.

The rest of the race was a long-drawn-out affair in light spotty air but exciting to us, since we kept widening out. *Nefertiti* and *Columbia* had started 15 minutes ahead of us, but the wind shift had so helped us that we were first at the mark. *Eagle* was right among the other two boats and at one time dropped to last before repassing *Columbia*. When we won eventually by 11 minutes, 42 seconds, it was a record win in any final trial race and one which was accompanied by a terrific din from the spectator fleet. The breaks had gone our way, as so often is the case for the boat ahead, but it was a great win and one bound to cause some panic in the *Eagle* camp.

↑
Pre-start circling in a final trial race against "Eagle". Neither boat gained an advantage. Note the gently curving wakes. It is important to keep good headway and not stall out by too sharp a turn.

A typical final trials start. Cox has timed it perfectly at the weather end. We have clear air and good headway a fourth of the way down the starting line. →

One minute after the preceding picture. We are driving prior to squeezing up. "Eagle" is already squeezing to avoid our backwind and is slowing down. A few minutes later we had worked up enough under her lee to force her about.

Any overconfidence we might have built up was stifled by a tight race with *Nefertiti* the next day. Ted Hood edged me at the start, on our leeward bow, and in 13 minutes of sailing gained one length on *Constellation*. In retrospect, I now feel we must have been feeling backwind despite being a length to windward. When *Nefertiti* tacked, we tacked short and within minutes had worked up enough to backwind her. From then on it was a question of *Constellation* widening out steadily, to win by 2 minutes, 18 seconds. The first couple of miles of that race, however, must have been exciting ones for Ted Hood and his gang. Just when any real hopes for success must have evaporated, those 2 miles opened the door to dreams. I almost found myself sorry to dash those hopes as soon as the first tack was made. We never looked like a loser thereafter, but the relatively small margin of victory, coupled with a 5-minute win by *Eagle* over *Columbia* in the other match, made us think that our big win over *Eagle* the day before was a bit of a fluke.

Next day's pairings matched us again with *Columbia,* while *American Eagle* took on *Nefertiti.* I doubt if anyone on any of the four boats failed to realize that if both older boats were to lose again, the field would be down to two. Any feelings of compassion I might have had during our race with *Nefertiti* (after we knew we had it won) were absent while maneuvering for the start. Our first goal all summer had been to get into the final pairing, and here was a chance to eliminate one contender while *Eagle,* hopefully, took care of the other. The fact that we liked Walter Podolak and his fine all-California crew had no effect on the killer instinct we felt as we pounced on *Columbia* with 8 minutes to go before the start. The circling in the 9-knot wind resulted in our getting the upper hand, and we crossed the line 16 seconds ahead of her and moving faster.

It was a routine race thereafter, with *Constellation* widening out on each leg except one reach when *Columbia* brought up a breeze from astern. The margin at the finish was over 5 minutes in a freshening wind.

In the other race, *Eagle* pinned a 4-minute loss on *Nefertiti.*

That evening back in harbor, we saw the Selection Committee calling on both *Nefertiti* and *Columbia.* They were expecting them and needed no guesses as to the purpose of their visit. We packed up our gear, put *Constellation* to bed real fast and beat it for Castle Hill before the Committee had reached *Columbia,* which was sharing our dock. We didn't want to be there when they got the bad news telling them that a summer's effort had come to an end.

But was it really a failure? In the narrow sense, yes, since their goal was to be chosen to defend the America's Cup. In the broader sense, however, they had been in many keen races, had seen their skills develop and could, I hope, take satisfaction from the fact that their being there had sharpened up both *Eagle* and *Constellation.* As a result, they had the thrill of sailing real thoroughbred boats in trials for *the* classic sailing event.

The above are thoughts which come to one only in retrospect. At the time, I'm sure they felt only disappointment even though their elimination was expected. I know I felt no elation as I drove back to the Hill. Any joy was confined to the area of thankfulness it wasn't us. In June it would have been a thrill to be one of two boats left in the fight. Now we felt some satisfaction for ourselves but more compassion for those for whom there was no tomorrow.

That evening we had a call from Ted Hood offering us any of his sails we might want, and the next morning got a similar offer from Walter Podolak. All of them were very philosophical about their elimination. When we commiserated with Ted, he made one of his longer speeches: "Oh, we knew it was coming." He also knew they had sailed well, had put in maximum effort, and that better boats had beaten them. The Californians were equally good sports, but seemed to blame themselves more. They had started too late, with too little and had put less time into it. Pat Dougan expressed it well by saying they had learned a lot. My guess is he will be back, with a better effort and a better boat.

That same evening we received a terse note from the Selection Committee notifying us about what we already knew and advising us to be prepared to meet *American Eagle* "tomorrow morning." We had won Round One. Now the *final* finals were about to begin.

"Constellation's" battle cry as flown by some of our more enthusiastic rooters and syndicate members.

Breaking *Eagle*'s Heart

American Eagle Was Never the Same after *Constellation* Came from Behind

I T FELT LONELY the next morning towing out to the America's Cup buoy. We missed *Nefertiti* and her stubby tender *King Tut*. We missed *Columbia* and her sleek tender loaded with enthusiastic Californians flying the California Bear flag. After months of meeting them, often in close racing, they were gone. Three straight losses in the final trial races and for them the end of the trial.

It made us realize the finality of the races we were now engaged in. We had one thing going for us, since in our first race against *American Eagle* in the final trials we had won big. A win today would give us a good edge, and even with a loss we would still be all even. It was just like the second game of the World Series.

By now we all had confidence in *Constellation* and in each other. The memory of those early losses against *Eagle* kept running through my mind as I went below and tried to catch a catnap lying on the stopped jibs in one of the sail bins. I had raced against *Eagle*'s skipper, Bill Cox, in many classes for more than twenty years and somewhat more often than not had come out second best. Now we were locked in the biggest battle of all, and I was running a bit scared.

A reduction in towing speed told me and the rest of the crew lolling below that we were at the buoy. We joined the others on deck, unstopped the main, attached the halyard and hauled up our favorite mainsail—our "winning main," as we were beginning to refer to it. Fenny and Dick cast off the tow line from *Chaperone* and we were on .our own, gliding quietly along at 6 knots under main alone.

What a day for sailing! Warm, clear and a 7-knot southerly which showed signs of picking up.

As we threaded our way through the spectator fleet of more than a hundred boats, I went forward to join our foredeck gang of Buddy Bombard, veteran of two Cup campaigns, Dick Goennel and Fenny Johnson. Bikini-clad girls kept waving at Buddy, who knows just about everyone, and their salutation of "Hi, Buddy" was invariably mimicked in falsetto tones by all the crew. Several boats owned by our supporters were flying huge flags bearing the bold message "Beat the Bird." One in the enemy camp flew one reading "Jar the Star." Nice to be taken so seriously.

Our small talk was doing a pretty fair job of quelling the butterflies which always came to me before a big race, when I noticed the Committee boat dropping anchor. It was 1130, half an hour before our scheduled start. Time to go aft and check the line, wind direction and to confer on what jib to set. "Dazzle 'em at the start, Reynard," was Buddy's parting remark. "Sure, no problem at all," I answered weakly, "but let's be a bit conservative on the line sighter." I still remembered being over the line early on the New York Yacht Club Cruise and now that we suspected *Constellation* was a bit faster than *Eagle*, I wanted above all not to be over early. Just give us good clear air and let us wind up approximately even on the line and I'll be happy.

Back in the cockpit, Eric Ridder, Rod Stephens and I had a brief conference on which jib to start with. If the present 7-knot wind held, it would be 3-ounce weather. A knot or two more and we would need the 5-ounce. We decided to gamble on the 3-ounce, hoping it would give us an early jump before the wind increased. Once ahead, we could probably switch, if need be, without losing our lead.

Eric ran the line while Rod and I read the two compasses. Then a check of the wind showed the windward end favored 2°. "Damn, I wish it favored the leeward end," I said. "Forget it," said Rod. No further comment. We all knew that *Constellation* was favored by being to leeward since being so incredibly close-winded, she could usually squeeze up and backwind *Eagle* if her bow was out front at the start. Favoring the windward end made this position less desirable. I decided to go for it anyway if we saw a clear shot for it. If not, and *Eagle* got to leeward of us, the line angle would compensate for our not having our favorite position. "Nothing to worry about," I thought to myself—believing not a single word of it.

Right on the dot of 1140 a gun barked, and course signals were hoisted smartly on the Committee boat *Alicia.* "Course 225°," they said, meaning the direction of the first mark, 4½ miles upwind. We knew from this the direction of the reaching mark 135° to port, and the course back to the starting buoy before again going to the windward mark, then running back to the start prior to a final beat where the finish would be set as the original first mark. Six legs in all—a beat, reach, reach, beat, run, beat, for a total of 24.3 miles. Plenty of drill for the crew, plenty of opportunity for changes in position if helmsman or crew pulled a rock.

As Rod scrambled below to lay out the course directions before posting them in clear view in the cockpit, I climbed over the traveler horse, took the wheel while Eric muttered, "Go get 'em, Bob," and took his station by the backstay winches.

"Check the intercom, Rod," I said—more to get something comfortable to think about than for any real need. It had been already checked on the way out, but there was something cheery about hearing Buddy's voice crackle through from the bow: "Hear you loud and clear. How are things on the dry end?"

Running the line, I noted it took us 2 minutes, 10 seconds under main alone—probably 1 minute, 50 seconds if we had jib on—vital information should we be running the line at the start.

The word was passed forward about our jib choice and with 15 minutes to go, our No. 1 3-ounce was hoisted in stops. "Lead number 26," I called to Don Wakeman, who had already checked the board and was in the process of setting the genoa slide in that very hole. "Set in lead 26," he replied.

"Five-ounce No. 2 in the chute, Buddy," Rod called forward on the intercom, "and make sure the ¾-ounce 45 is ready." The ¾-ounce 45 was our favorite spinnaker for this weight of wind. We all knew it was already flaked down in one of the spinnaker bunks, ready to hook on at a moment's notice. Seven other spinnakers were also ready, but Rod's warning gave the foredeck gang some indication of priority so that the 45-foot would be one of four most accessible chutes.

Constellation felt lively as we reached back and forth below the line.

Eagle was keeping her distance off beyond the leeward extension. Glad Bill doesn't want to hook up too early.

My mouth was getting dry already. "Got some gum, Steve?" I asked, and Steve Van Dyck, our twenty-one-year-old coffee grinder tailer and spinnaker sheet man, immediately produced two sticks.

Our watches showed the 10-minute gun approaching. Rod and Eric each carried back-up watches and I used a wrist stop watch, preferring to refer to it rather than have time called. All three were stopped and reset to zero in order to time the warning gun exactly.

We saw the smoke, and a split second later heard the gun's bang. Rod hollered "10 minutes" to the crew, not because they didn't know it but because experience had taught us that occasionally someone got mixed up on the time remaining. *Eagle* was off beyond the buoy end of the line and tacking back toward us as we cleared the Committee boat and reached for a spot 100 yards to leeward of the buoy. In a bit more than a minute, if both boats held course, we should meet about 100 yards to leeward of the line and near its mid-point. Just right as far as position, I thought, but if we hook up there, it will mean nearly 8 minutes of exhausting tailing. "We will hook up as we come together," I shouted so all could hear. No complaints even by a glance. All hands knew these races were for real, and I especially wanted to start the circling process at the mid-point of the line, where there was less chance of being blocked should *Eagle* get on our tail.

The next minute was the hard one. Little to do except think and chew gum as the two boats closed. I bore off slightly in hopes of getting further to leeward of *Eagle* so we could later sharpen up and end our approach on a higher than reciprocal course. No dice. Bill Cox, as expected, bore off to an exact reciprocal. We would pass about 100 feet apart.

Now *Eagle* was only 100 yards ahead, and we were closing at a combined rate of 12 knots. "Break jib," I called, and Bob Connell and Fred Kulicke spun the coffee grinders, the jib stops broke and the big sail snapped full with a dull pop. *American Eagle*'s jib broke out seconds later. We would surely hook up as we passed. The speedometers showed speed increasing gradually—6.1, 6.3, and just as we came bow to bow with *Eagle,* over 7.

Now was the crucial moment. Proper timing of our swing might get us on her tail or at least keep *Eagle* from getting on ours. Just as the bows overlapped, I spun the wheel. Cox spun *Eagle*'s at the same instant. If either had delayed, it would have given the other a real advantage.

We shot head to wind, the jib slotted over, the coffee grinders spun and all sails snapped full. *Eagle* had completed her jibe and was exactly where we had been 20 seconds before, and *Constellation* was sailing in *Eagle*'s old position. We were still all even, neither having gained an advantage, neither lost.

I eased the helm to let her gain headway before jibing, hollered for main to be eased and kept one eye on *Eagle*, the other on the speedometer. She was trimming main furiously, sharpening up and no longer on an exact reciprocal course. "Don't rush it, Bob," I told myself. "Better to bear off slowly and then spin through the jibe with full headway." I had learned the hard way that it usually worked better that way. But it wasn't easy to watch *Eagle* swinging up faster than we were bearing off.

Six knots on the speedometer. Fast enough. "Ease main," I shouted, and moments later spun the wheel hard over. No need to tell the crew "jibe" or other colorful lingo. They had been here before. They knew what was coming. Larry rushed aft and helped Rod pull the three-part main sheet over in two great heaves. No need to run the sheet through blocks in this weight of wind. She came faster if jibed all standing. As the boom swung over, great bights of main sheet smacked across the cockpit. Eric ducked, I swung my head back from the wheel and it was clear, dropping in the water for a second before the sail filled on the new tack and the sheet was snapped taut, small drops of water springing from it into the sea. Funny the small things you notice at a moment like this!

"Now trim!!!!" As though it were necessary to tell this crew what to do. Larry was already back at his winch, tailing, as Fenny heaved the main in hand over hand. Dick and Buddy had the winch handle in place, ready to grind her in once Fenny could no longer trim with muscle alone.

The sheet was sucking through the blocks, but oh, to have it even faster—*Constellation* was ready to go, go higher, but had to wait for the main. Now the sheet was on the winch, Fenny still grappling with it but backed up by the enormous but slower power of the Barient. Bob Connell on the coffee grinder was able, with relative ease, to keep the genoa full as we slowly arched closer to the wind. Seven knots on the speedometer, and nearly on the wind. Time to spin her over. No words had been spoken—none now as we tacked. Everyone knew what was next, and as we eased into the wind, Don cast off the leeward jib sheet after letting the genoa back for an instant to accelerate our swing.

Fenny dropped to the deck for a few seconds' rest, Dick and Buddy stopped grinding and followed suit, and it was Steve's turn to put out as he grabbed fathom after fathom of line to bring the big jib around. Freddy started flailing at the coffee grinder, Larry watched, ready to ease main as soon as it was full.

"One minute, 10 seconds, Bob," said Eric, who had been checking the time it took to complete a circle. Five minutes, 10 seconds to go. Time for two more circles anyway.

Eagle had managed to gain ever so slightly. Now as we passed, instead of being on reciprocal courses she was perhaps 10° closer to being on our tail than we to hers. When we completed our second circle at the 4-minute mark, she had gained perhaps another 5°, due perhaps to her larger rudder, which enabled bearing off a shade faster. Nothing to worry about really, because she was far from being able to block us from tacking or jibing.

There was less than 3 minutes as we completed our third circle, which meant it would be about 2:20 when the forthcoming jibe had been made. "What do you think of going for it after jibing?" I queried. "Yes," was Rod's only comment. "O.K.," said Eric. The whole success of the start hinged on this decision. I would have liked it to be a bit later, as we would surely be early if we jibed and went for it full bore.

We made a slower jibe than usual to get a bit further from the line, and once the sail came over, I hollered "slow trim," welcome news to Fenny. Headway was killed slightly. Now if only *Eagle* will jibe in our wake. We can kill enough to keep from being early, and if she attempts to pass, can speed up and possibly force her over the line early.

No such luck—hadn't expected her to anyway. Instead of jibing, *Eagle* reached away from the line. It was obvious she would tack for the windward end and have full headway at the gun.

We could reach off for the leeward end and cross with full way too, but I hated to be separated by the full length of the line. It just didn't make sense to be so far apart in a boat which was a trifle faster. "Trim hard," I shouted to Fenny, who gave me a "What the hell now" look as he grabbed the sheet. "Ready about," and two seconds later, "Hard alee," followed by "Trim for on the wind." My plan was to approach the Committee boat end on port tack, then tack on to starboard to cross, with hopes of getting a safe leeward.

We seemed to take forever to gain headway. I could see *Eagle* tacking on our leeward bow and a moment later reaching directly for us, flat out. We were still only up to 6 knots. Can't wait any longer or *Eagle* will overrun us. "Forty-five seconds," Rod called. I spun the wheel and tacked. With 30 seconds to go, we were on the wind, down to 4.8 knots and with *Eagle* on our weather quarter with a real bone in her teeth.

Since she was a length to windward of us, we couldn't slow her down by backwind. Would we pick up headway fast enough to keep our wind clear? It would be close and the whole race might hinge on it. My wish to keep close to *Eagle* had not included being close behind!

Twenty seconds to go, speed up to 6 knots, but *Eagle* still gaining and now just one length behind. On the intercom I heard Buddy announce, "Two lengths from the line, closing fast," just as my watch read 15 seconds. Better drive off a shade and we may need to anyway, to keep wind clear. At 10 seconds it was reassuring to hear Buddy call "Charge," our word for go for the line—you won't be early. *Eagle* was charging too, was overlapping us, her bow abreast our cockpit and still creeping up. As usual, Bill had a perfectly timed start, *Eagle's* genoa blocking out the white flag mere seconds after the gun.

I squeezed against the cockpit coaming, watched the jib for the slightest break, and called "Ease 3 inches" to Don. Speed now over 7. A glance to windward showed *Eagle's* bow was now abreast our mast but no longer rushing past. "Bearing 285°," said Rod, "distance 30 yards." A minute later: "Bearing 283°, distance 35." Not good, but speed now 7.5 knots. A minute later: "Bearing 285°, distance 40."

Good—now we could go to work. We still had our bow in front by the length of our foredeck. *Eagle* had edged us at the start, but we were safe and while we would have preferred to be half the distance to leeward, we were in our favorite spot on her lee bow. Eric saw me chewing gum as if to tear it apart and offered me a cigarette. As I reached to grab it, I could see *Eagle* dropping back ever so slightly. "Trim jib," I said to Don, but not bothering to say how much, because he well knew where we liked it in this much breeze. *Constellation* was dancing now and our spirits danced too as Rod called, "Bearing 289°, distance same."A couple of minutes later it was 289°, distance 35, followed at regular intervals by 290° and 32, 295° and 30.

Too close now to get distance readings, and the bearing could be checked by eye. Time to squeeze up, I thought, and Eric echoed it by saying, "You can squeeze now." I brought our head up slightly. Speed dropped 3/10 of a knot, but we were closing the gap. *Eagle*'s shadow marched up our deck, then paused. Squeeze a bit more. Down to 6.5, but still her shadow hung. She was squeezing too, trying to keep clear of our backwind but not liking it sailing so high. Then her shadow started creeping aft, and a glance to windward showed her bow opposite our wheel. We had her!

Eagle's tack came as I was watching. We held on for a length, the crew getting ready for the tack they knew was coming, then with only the words "hard alee" being spoken, we arched slowly through the eye of the wind, and on to port tack.

"A wide trim," I called to Steve, who was tailing the genoa and could hear Rod calling to Larry to ease main. Now we had to go. *Eagle* had eased even more and was going hell bent to the west. In a few moments we were up to 7.8 knots—plenty fast enough for the 7-knot wind, yet *Eagle* had sagged off and was a good three lengths to leeward with our bow almost overlapping her stern. We eased jib a few more inches, and as we did could see *Eagle* trimming slightly. Bearing 290°, distance 80—then 295°, 80; 300°, 80; 305°, 82. We were going by and Rod allowed himself the first pat of the day, reaching over the side and giving *Constellation*'s topside a couple of love taps.

With Rod, a good boat is a living thing—made up of wood, steel, engineering and technical know-how, but evolving not as a machine but as something alive. And not just any old being either, but one to be appreciated.

We were abeam of *Eagle* when she tacked. A bit earlier than I had anticipated and our covering tack was a couple of seconds slow in starting. In hopes of blanketing, I swung too fast. We wound up almost, but not quite, on her wind and our quick swing had killed our way. *Eagle* tacked back, and this time we held until we had good headway and gained nicely when we came around. There were two lengths of water between us as she crossed our stern on the next tack, but now *Eagle* was out of phase and we could no longer tack on her. No matter, I thought, we were easing out ahead ever so slightly on each tack, and with a half hour gone, *Constellation* was looking mighty good.

Seven miles from the start. We flew down the reaching leg, both boats trimmed to perfection, neither one gaining on the other.

Then it happened. *Eagle* had tacked onto port, and as we crossed her bow by five lengths, we ran into a real flat spot—3 or 4 knots at best. Speed was over 7 knots, but as I tacked on *Eagle*'s weather bow, we dropped down to 4 knots. Just then *Eagle* entered the flat but was generating her own apparent wind strength and kept flying through it.

We eased everything but just didn't have enough headway to pick up more than 5 knots in the dying breeze. In a couple of minutes the wind came back, but by then *Eagle* had driven through and was out on our leeward bow—and ahead.

It wasn't until later that evening, in fact, that it dawned on me what had gone wrong and that I realized that no matter what the tactical situation called for, it was sudden death to tack a big heavy Twelve to cover in the middle of a hole in the wind. All I realized at the time was that our comfortable lead had evaporated in two minutes' time and we were behind a boat which had shown every sign of going slower.

I was mad, mad only at myself, and even madder thereby. Halfway up the weather leg we were behind and *Eagle* was off to the west of us with every likelihood of the wind hauling to the west.

When she came about, we were unable to cross but could get a safe leeward. *Eagle* tacked clear, and next time when we came together we were again unable to cross. I realized later we should have gone under her stern, but at the moment kept thinking the third time we could surely cross. I had not reasoned with the westerly shift which kept *Eagle* almost even with us.

Approaching the mark on port tack, we had gained almost enough to cross. For a moment I thought we could, but Rod, who had been taking bearings, fairly shouted, "Go under." He later admitted he too *thought* we could cross, but we had a long standing agreement that unless we were *sure*, we would never press matters in the early stage of a race. After all, we had five legs to go.

Still I was pretty mad at myself as we rounded 12 seconds behind at the end of 4½ miles of sailing.

Spinnakers on both boats were hoisted smartly and were drawing almost as soon as the sterns had cleared the tug. We got our spinnaker staysail up first and lit off for the reaching mark 3½ miles away. Wind had increased and we were making 9 knots on the speedometer. But we were not making or losing an inch on *Eagle*. We flew down the leg as one, locked in with a length of open water between.

"Eagle" jibed wide to take the second mark close aboard on the new course. We are about to follow suit. Both jibes were flawless and we remained the same distance behind.

Both boats jibed perfectly without the big chutes collapsing for so much as an instant. On the second reach we held a bit high, gained slightly as we drew up on *Eagle*'s quarter but lost it back as we bore off for the mark. On the second reach we had switched to our 5-ounce jib, and were disappointed to see *Eagle* breaking out the same weight sail. We would have to catch them with equal weapons, and it didn't look too promising as we rounded 17 seconds behind.

The chute had come down just before the mark, and as we rounded I called forward, "Tell me when we can tack." The reply was instantaneous—"Ready to tack." It didn't seem possible all the mess of lines could be cleared up so fast, but because it had, we swung around the buoy onto port tack and into clear air. *Eagle* followed immediately—a good clearing job there too, but they did have 20 seconds more to do so.

We were bow to bow now, but two lengths to leeward. Even worse, we were running into greater slop from the spectator fleet, and *Constellation* felt dead. She looked it, too, as *Eagle* drove past. After two minutes we had to tack to clear our wind, a process soon repeated many times. Each time *Eagle* would drive off on us, and since her bow was always ahead, there was no opportunity to squeeze up without getting blanketed.

Three quick tacks finally got our wind clear with our bow in front, and finally we began to gain. We were, however, perilously close to the lay line and would have to catch her before reaching it. No dice. We were still a length to leeward when we reached the lay line. *Eagle* overstood on purpose, waiting for us to tack and hoping to pounce on us. On and on we went, gaining ever so slightly, but all would hinge on whether we could manage clear air on the opposite tack.

Rod, Eric and I decided on a sneak tack, passed the word forward, and I spun the wheel hard before a man had moved. *Eagle* was ready and tacked almost with us. We had clear air, were fetching, but could we hold it? *Eagle*'s bow was nearly half a length in front, and as we drove off below the mark, she drove off with us. Rod and Eric screamed at them to keep up, I piped up too, but the damage was done. We had to come up to make the mark, and as we did, *Eagle* was directly on our wind.

Nothing to do but grit our teeth and bear it and plan for the running leg. It was a dead run, but we elected to jibe as soon as rounding, expecting *Eagle* to set on the starboard jibe. She was a long-looking

7 lengths and 45 seconds ahead as she rounded, but thank God she was setting to starboard.

We could see seas from the spectator fleet rolling *Eagle* about and collapsing her spinnaker as she squared off for the leeward mark. Our ¾-ounce 45 blossomed out to port, and we held a good 30° high to get her moving. And move she did. Within minutes we had halved the distance as *Eagle* jibed to cover and reached through our wind shadow.

All down the leg we jibed, crossing *Eagle*'s stern at least ten times, and each time we crossed, it was a shade closer. The wind had picked up to 13 or 14 knots. It was gorgeous sailing, but we had little chance to appreciate the beauty of it. We did enjoy watching Bill Cox looking back nervously. It's easier to be behind and coming, but still we would have traded places if only we could. For a while it looked like we might go by before the mark, but still there was two lengths between us as *Eagle* dropped her chute and prepared to jibe.

"Carry chute to the mark and take it down to starboard as we jibe," was the word we passed forward. It was risky because we would need to tack at once to clear our wind, and a late douse made this almost impossible. We had practiced this maneuver dozens of times all summer and occasionally were able to douse, jibe and then tack almost in one fluid motion. Now was the time it *had* to work.

The spinnaker was still partly up as the main boom swung over and our bow passed the mark. Buddy was shouting, "You can tack," while the mast was abreast of it, and with a grin and a prayer I let her come up and over onto port. Lines were everywhere, being dragged around with the genoa sheet as we swung through the wind. Dick, Fenny and Buddy swarmed around the foredeck, yanking spinnaker sheet and guys clear and following the genoa clew around the mast and leeward shrouds. She came home, festooned with a veritable bucket of worms, but home she was and we were clear. *Eagle* was abaft our beam and *Constellation* had clearly gained. Then the spectator wash began to kill us again, just as it had more than an hour before when in this same spot. We had to get out of there but fast, but couldn't until all the spinnaker gear was cleared up and out of the way.

On the leeward leg our council of war had resulted in a decision to short-tack repeatedly—the entire leg if need be—in hopes of wearing *Eagle* down. Not much hope in doing what we had last time upwind even though it had so nearly worked. As long as we could gain or hold even, we would instead tack and keep on tacking.

First we had to get out of phase to keep from being blanketed as *Eagle* tacked on top. "Three quick ones," I called and then brought her up in the wind. *Eagle* was ready and tacked right on us, but no sooner had we filled away than we tacked back. *Eagle* held on to gather headway, and when she tacked to starboard, we tacked almost instantly to port.

We were going slow now, little over 4 knots, and *Eagle* had opened up a four-length lead by waiting for headway before tacking. We had traded two lengths for being on the opposite tack and from here on she could never tack on us, provided we tacked at the same instant.

Eagle tacked back to port earlier than we would have wished, because we still hadn't regained as much headway. We tacked anyway and were pleased to sense that we lost nothing on the last exchange. "They have a different jib on!" exclaimed Eric. And sure enough their 5-ounce had been shifted to a heavier one. The wind was now 14 knots —O.K. for a heavy jib if the boat were settled down on a course, but not so hot in short tacking when maximum drive was needed to regain headway. The glow of this realization was just flooding over us when Eric announced *Eagle* was tacking again.

"Hard alee," I called and slowly, ever so slowly, I brought her head up. We had regained full speed by now and I knew that *Constellation* loved a long loping tack. The cast-off was perfect, we shot into the wind, lazily swung off as Bob Connell, Freddy, Larry and Fenny pawed the deck, spun the linked coffee grinders with flailing arms and had her sheeted fully home just as we reached a full and by course. We had dropped only from 8 knots to 6.5 during the tack and had shot to windward.

Rod had the stadimeter going and called "130 yards" as we crossed *Eagle*'s stern. A bad margin, but we knew we had gained. She tacked square on our wind and we tacked away, with the same deliberate motion the four men grimacing and grunting at the winches, the tailer flailing at the genoa sheet. "One hundred twenty yards," Rod fairly shouted as we crossed next time. Three and a half miles to go! We could catch them yet.

The tacks were coming every minute or two now, Buddy and Dick were taking their turns at the coffee grinders while two men grabbed a rest. Even so, it made me wonder just how much more they could take. "How you guys doing?" I shouted. "Give us a hundred more," Bob

Connell, who had never been spelled, bellowed back. They had heard Rod calling ranges of 110, 100, 90, 83, 75 and finally 55 yards. They, too, could take time to look ahead at the ever-closing gap.

Two miles to go. Up ahead I could see Bill crouching ever lower over the wheel, casting quick glances to leeward as he crossed us, glancing at the main, the seas to windward and back again to us. Always back to us. I saw him swing up sharply this time—too sharply. He was making the same mistake I had on the first windward leg. Sure enough, as we swung through our tack I could see *Eagle* full and by on her main with her genoa still not sheeted home yet. "Slow and easy now, Bob," I muttered half aloud. "Thirty-five yards," hollered Rod.

On the next tack we were even closer—too close for Rod to get stadimeter readings. Still he held it up, appeared to take a reading and, facing toward *Eagle*, shouted, "Another 10 yards, Bob." On the next tack it was, "Cut it in half again, Bob." It dawned on me these readings were not for me but for Bill Cox, to give him all possible worry.

And plenty of worry he had! As we tacked to starboard, we were a bare 20 yards astern. A moment later we matched *Eagle*'s tack and drove off onto port tack. She was crossing us by less than a length and *Constellation* was smashing through the seas, throwing spray and exuding power. We were up to 8 knots as *Eagle* crossed us—too close to tack on top.

"This time we hold," I shouted, not caring if *Eagle* heard. The crew dropped on deck, stacked up like so many logs, their faces trained on *Eagle* as she tacked broad off our weather bow. We were abeam when she was sheeted home and we were flying. "All full," our crew shouted in derision, and then "bye-bye" accompanied by eight hands waving at our desperate foe. We all knew this was it, all knew we would drive through and stay there.

Eagle hung on grimly, but in 2 minutes which seemed like an hour, we squeezed up under her bow, forced her to tack and followed suit a moment later. There was a mile to go and we led by only 50 feet, but *Constellation* was moving. The wind had died slightly and *Eagle*'s heavier jib was doing her no good, while ours looked like sculptured perfection. Within 5 minutes we were on her wind, gained more when she tacked three times to get out of phase and applied a loose cover thereafter.

No one said much during that last mile. Rod and I both gave *Constellation* a loving pat, but when we crossed at 17:36, the spectator fleet

tore the air apart. Everyone was jumping up and down as though possessed, and our gang on *Chaperone* went into a combination war dance and hugfest.

But it was all nothing compared to what went on in *Constellation*. The crew leapt into the cockpit howling like wolves, grabbing at my hand, Eric's, Rod's, pounding each other and all eleven of us talking, shouting and screaming at once.

We were quiet when *Eagle* crossed 1 minute, 8 seconds later, then broke into a rousing cheer as the spectator horns spoke again with equal volume. No jumping or waving greeted her, and on *Eagle* the crow slowly got to their feet, lowered jib and walked aimlessly about.

I climbed over the main traveler horse, jumped into the main cockpit as Rod threaded us through the beaming spectator fleet. I saw Charlotte throw me a kiss, saw her face half beaming, half crying; and realized I was doing almost the same right back at her.

Suddenly I felt tired. For over 4 hours I hadn't noticed the slightest fatigue. Now my knees were literally shaking and as I sat on deck, feet draped into the cockpit, I found it just a bit hard to draw an even breath.

A moment later, with a beer in hand, I found I began reliving the past 4½ hours, all compressed into a minute's thought. The many mistakes I had made on that first leg flashed before me, the long chase condensed itself into seconds and finally as I thought of that last leg I found myself smiling.

Suddenly I realized that the long uphill battle of the summer was all but over. Suddenly my fear of *Eagle* and Bill Cox semed to float away. Bill, except on that last leg, had sailed an almost flawless race. I had not, but we had never given up, never cracked and finally had done what had to be done. I would not likely make the same mistake a second time. Bill could hardly expect to sail so well again. And both *Constellation* and her crew could be counted on when the going got toughest.

Rod looked at me quizzically as he caught me smiling to myself, perhaps not realizing that it was at that very moment I knew that it was now anly a matter of time before we would be chosen to defend the America's Cup.

After breathing down "Eagle's" neck for twenty miles "Constellation" finally broke through. "Eagle" was never quite the same thereafter.

Selected!

WHILE WE MIGHT have broken *Eagle*'s heart in the second trial race, we didn't kill their determination. The race on Saturday, August 22, was called because of fog. Sunday was a lay day. The ensuing ten days, August 24–September 2, were as pressure-packed as any I've experienced. Strangely, the pressure mounted with each victory, as we got ever closer to the goal we wanted so much, had sought so long.

The race on Monday started in 8 knots, got up to 14 at times. Cox edged me at the start with a safe leeward, but we tacked and within 10 minutes we were backwinding *Eagle*. Our lead was 1 minute, 19 seconds at the weather mark. We lost a bit on the reaches to start upwind the second time just over a minute ahead. The sea was more lumpy now, the wind stronger and we flew upwind, flew on the run and again on the final thrash upwind, giving *Eagle* a loose cover throughout. We were over 4 minutes ahead at the finish, which in the growing breeze represented 1200 yards in distance.

While towing in, some of the younger crew members started conjecture about the possibility of our being selected that night. Eric, Rod and I all insisted, "Not a chance." And we meant it. But there was just a glimmer of hope. Apparently some reporters believed there was a possibility of selection that evening, because more of them than usual were at our dock. We knew that the Selection Committee was waiting for a fresh breeze to test us in, knew also that three straight wins, however convincing, were too few on which to base selection. They probably felt *Eagle* might rebound, though her losses were due not so much to a decline on *Eagle*'s part as on a great improvement on ours. If we could just keep on sailing well, we had 'em.

On Tuesday, August 25, Bill Cox requested a lay day and was

granted it. The purpose was to give him a chance to try a new mainsail and do other recutting. I couldn't blame Bill for asking, but we were all surprised and a bit miffed to see his request granted. We had understood that once the final trials began, we were to be prepared to race each day, with breakdowns being the only justification for postponement. After all, hadn't we all had four months in which to buy, test and recut sails?

Bill Cox, however, is a very persuasive fellow, and he got his lay day. It gave the *Eagle* crew more than time to try new sails, they also had a chance to realign their thinking, to make changes and just by doing something, to bolster their sinking confidence. We had little to do and hence took half the day off, turning up en masse at Bailey Beach.

The race scheduled for Wednesday, the 26th, was canceled by fog, but it was clear and blowing 6 knots on Thursday, the 27th. I don't know how Cox and his gang felt, but I was more nervous after our two days of rest. I kept worrying if Bill had discovered something.

We got edged at the start but had good clear air on *Eagle*'s leeward bow. From this position it took us 11 minutes to work up enough to force *Eagle* about. Thereafter it remained close, but with *Constellation* widening out slowly but steadily. We won finally by nearly 3 minutes.

Again the conjecture about selection that night, but still we considered it most unlikely, since we had won again in light air, a breeze in which we had by now established our superiority. When we saw the Selection Committee head home, we followed suit.

Friday, August 28, was a great day for sailing, with 12 to 14 knots of wind at the start and the chance of more to come. This was the strongest wind we had met *Eagle* in. This one we *had* to win. Our prospects looked poor at first when Bill got on our tail. With three minutes to go, we headed to leeward of the Committee boat with *Eagle* a bit over one length astern. We headed up as though to tack, and at this instant *Eagle* shot to windward of the Committee boat, hoping to block us off and force us to windward of the line. I had been half expecting this and hence did not complete our tack. *Eagle* had to in order to clear the Committee boat, and hence with a minute and a half to go, we were on opposite tacks and free to call our own shots. We bore off in a slow circle, jibed and came roaring for the weather end of the line with full headway. *Eagle* had to jibe, then tack and crossed two

Peter and his crew of "Sovereign" are all eyes as "Constellation" and "Eagle" battle it out in the final trials. "Eagle" is threatening here but she never passed. We rounded the mark 29 seconds ahead, then opened out on the windward leg.

lengths to leeward of us. She crossed 6 seconds ahead of us, but we, by being at the favored end and going faster, had a slight edge.

We now had such confidence in *Constellation* that I expected to eat out from this vantage point. We did, but oh, so slightly, and 4½ miles later were only 20 seconds ahead, with *Eagle*'s best point of sailing coming up. We gained 14 seconds on the first reach by sailing a more direct course, then lost 5 seconds on the next reach, to start upwind again 29 seconds ahead. We suspected our mediocre performance on the first beat had been caused by having a 9-ounce jib set and hence went to the 5-ounce. The improvement was dramatic and we were nearly 2 minutes ahead at the next mark and feeling pretty good.

We had a few anxious moments on the run when we went soft, but still rounded with more than a minute lead. Again we moved out on the beat, taking the growing seas in stride to win by 2 minutes, 5 seconds. It was a big win, since it proved we could take her in moderate going as well as light. Especially impressive was our ability to slice through the seas without hobbyhorsing—a trait demonstrated even more graphically in the heavy weather races against *Sovereign*.

This time when the talk started about possibly being selected that night, we didn't squash it. We said we didn't expect it, but I for one had a deep-down feeling that tonight was the night. *Eagle* had had her lay day and we had taken her twice since, as convincingly as before. We had won five straight in winds from 5 to 15 knots and had looked particularly good as the seas built up. Even if *Eagle* were now to win five in a row, we would still be all even and well into September, with little time left for the deciding races, little time to prepare for the defense itself. What more could the Selection Committee ask for?

We took our time clearing *Constellation* away, looking surreptitiously for that little blue launch which the Committee used. Reporters and cameramen were crowding the docks eager to record the climactic moment. Some were old friends like Ev Morris, John Rendel, Len Fowle, John Ahern, Stan Rosenfeld, and others. They ventured the opinion that we were "in." We made lame denials, really agreeing with them in our hearts. When the Committee launch was seen heading for her night's berth, we tried not to look surprised or indignant, but we didn't fool anyone.

There was considerable grousing at Castle Hill that night. "They must want to see us in a strong breeze," I remarked, then added, to myself, "But how long can you keep on beating Bill Cox, even in a boat you feel is a bit superior?" Knowing we couldn't win 'em all and realizing we were on the brink of selection actually intensified the pressure. In the *Eagle* camp, there was pressure too, plenty of it, because they must approach each race now knowing that one more loss and it could be all over.

Fog prevented another start until September 1, and lack of breeze could well have prevented it then. The Committee must have been anxious to get on with it too, however, as they sent us away in a 3-knot wind.

We got a fine start at the leeward end, with all the momentum that 5 minutes on one tack could give. And we were heading toward what appeared to be better air. *Eagle* was 9 seconds later getting across the line at the extreme other end. It looked good for us for all of 5 minutes. Then we saw a new wind coming in to windward, a wind *American Eagle* was sure to get first. She did, and it turned out to be a 90° shift too, turning the first leg into a reach. She eased by and rounded first by two lengths. We held even in the broad reach to the next mark. The third leg was now a beat and when we tacked to clear our air, *Eagle* held on. Bill was conceding our greater speed in light going and planned instead of covering to go where he considered best. Had he done that in the second trial race, we probably would not have caught him. We didn't this time, though we were still just two lengths astern at the third mark. The shortened course gave us only one reach to go, and in desperation we set spinnaker. It was a poor move and merely put us further behind, losing by just over 1 minute.

That evening there was no panic in our camp. We had lost a fluky race but had pressed throughout and, except for the choice of using a spinnaker on the last leg, had sailed a pretty good race. If we had to lose one, this was a good one to lose.

Next day was a beautiful day for sailing—12 knots and a fair-sized sea. As if by mutual agreement, we hooked up and started circling especially early, a full 12 minutes before the start. We could have avoided *Eagle* till later, but didn't want to appear to be running scared and hence came at her early. To our delight, we stayed even or even gained a bit in the circling, and with 6 minutes to go, it was apparent we were in no danger of being blocked. With a faster boat we had no desire to try to block her. Clear air and an even start was all we asked.

It couldn't have been more even. After making three more circles, we went for it, with *Eagle* on our weather quarter. I was afraid of being early, but *Eagle* was pressing and hence we kept going. Bill told me later they had the same fear but didn't want to let us get away. At the gun two horns sounded, two sets of numbers were hoisted. We had each sucked the other into getting over early, by inches.

Both boats bore off, dipped the line and swung up again, in exactly the same relative positions as at the gun, but further down the line, with us two lengths on their leeward bow.

Then we started the now familiar squeeze and in less than a mile had forced them about. When we tacked to cover, *Constellation* leaped ahead, slicing through the seas like a stiletto. We rounded 200 yards ahead, lost somewhat on the two reaches, but then really put the frosting on the cake the next time upwind. The wind had lightened but the seas were still there. They slowed us but they really murdered *American Eagle*.

The wind lightened to almost nothing, then came on and shifted, and throughout we managed to keep our foe covered. On the fifth leg we set our tiny 40-foot spinnaker, drew away handsomely and then shifted it as the wind came up, opening still more.

The last leg was a close reach under jib in a now solid breeze. On our way to the finish, we passed close aboard *Eagle* as she was going for the last mark. Bill waved gamely and we returned it somewhat quietly. This was no time to rub it in by too much of a display of jubilation. *Eagle* was a badly beaten boat, with no future in this race, and with probably no tomorrow.

Our margin at the finish was a full three quarters of a mile—4 minutes, 27 seconds in time. The last entry in the daily record read: "A real big win, which *should* do it."

It did! Within minutes after both boats arrived at their docks, we saw the Selection Committee heading in *Eagle*'s direction. I raced for a phone. Charlotte had had to miss the last two races (the only ones she missed all summer) due to an ear infection. The doctor left specific instructions that under no circumstances must she go downstairs or even get out of bed.

"The Selection Committee is heading toward *Eagle*," I blurted; "come on down here!" "I'm practically on my way," she cried, and I saw her minutes later elbowing her way down the dock which was

Happiest day of the summer. The selection committee has come aboard to announce that "Constellation" will defend the America's Cup.

overflowing with the whole town of Newport. Rob and Louise, who had seen the race, were already there, and the four of us stared in hushed expectancy as the blue launch pulled up alongside.

Harry Morgan hiked himself aboard, amid deafening silence, grabbed Eric's hand and said, "Mr. Ridder, I have the honor to inform you that *Constellation* has been chosen to defend the America's Cup."

If he said anything else, history will have to wait, because the silence was destroyed by a mighty shout first from our crew, a shout taken up by all hands on the dock. I hugged and kissed Charlotte and Louise, and got it back with interest. Rob broke into a big grin and we started pounding each other on the back. Pretty soon everyone was pounding everyone else and kissing every girl in sight. I shook hands with the Selection Committee, all friends and never better friends than at that moment. Champagne appeared as if by magic. Some got inside, some

Harold (Mike) Vanderbilt came aboard to offer congratulations, especially to Rod and Olin Stephens. All are three time America's Cup winners—Mike as skipper of "Enterprise" 1930, "Rainbow" 1934 and "Ranger" 1937; Rod as an invaluable crew on "Ranger", "Columbia" 1958 and "Constellation" 1964; Olin as the genius designer of "Ranger", "Columbia" and "Constellation".

Charlotte and I were mighty pleased with the world and with each other on the day of selection.

Tee and Eric Ridder were just as pleased as we were on the day the great news came.

Olin, Rod, Eric and I were not lacking in confidence as we huddled beneath "Constellation" a few days before the match with "Sovereign".

"Constellation's" winning combination: her skipper Eric Ridder, her builder Henry Sayers, designer Olin Stephens and her happy helmsman.

got sloshed on heads, some down fronts. It was a World's Series dressing room in a nautical setting.

Then we saw *Eagle*'s crew approaching, standing straight on their tender, with Bill Cox at the very bow. The noise, the horseplay stopped as if by command. Bill led them in a rousing cheer for *Constellation,* a cheer we screamed right back at them for *American Eagle.* It was easier for us to yell louder, not having such a big lump in our throats. If the one I had had been any bigger, I would have had trouble breathing. Here was a realization of a dream. We were going to race for the America's Cup. Yet before Bill and his fine crew I found the moment filled with sadness. Mine was the first hand Bill shook. He looked happier than I felt, and his "Nice going, Bob" had a real warmth to it. I probably said something inane and certainly inadequate in reply.

Then with new glasses of champagne in hand the mood changed and boisterous congratulations and backslapping were once more the order of the day.

The Selection Committee made a hasty exit, the two crews started talking over past races, not without a few insults mixed with offers of all possible help in the way of sails or anything else thrown in. They put up a brave show. For us it was easy.

In twenty minutes they climbed back on board their tender, shoved off with our heartfelt cheers ringing in their ears.

Castle Hill was a mad place that night. Charlotte wouldn't go to bed till midnight. When the doctor called the next day, he was amazed at her recovery and commended her for being such a good patient. There are more effective medicines than pills.

Two days later, after we had rushed home for a brief respite, we got word that *Sovereign* had been selected as challenger over *Kurrewa V.* I sent the following telegram to Peter Scott, "Congratulations to you and your crew. Second best news we have had this week."

It had been a climactic week, a week I felt no other could ever match in excitement. How could I then know the feeling which comes while towing out of Newport Harbor to race for the America's Cup? I found out on September 15, 1964.

We Defend the Cup!

ALL HANDS WENT HOME for a few days after our selection. I must admit it was fun to bask in the congratulations from friends who still seemed a bit incredulous that we had turned the tables on *American Eagle* so completely.

We were back in Newport nine days before the match. Practice was a bit less intense than before the final trials. We did work on our interim jib change and improved our time a bit more. We practiced jibes and other maneuvers just to keep our timing in. Most time, however, was spent practicing starts and checking and recutting sails.

For start practice I had the best in the business as opponents. Bus Mosbacher took *American Eagle* out for a couple of days, together with some of his old *Weatherly* gang. If he was rusty, he sure didn't show it and managed to beat me more often than not. These starts were not conservative. I welcomed hooking up beyond the extremities of the line, tried to block *Eagle* just as Bus tried to block me. It was a great help, and toward the end I did better. Another day, Ted Hood went at it with us, with all the intensity of real racing. Bus spent a day on *Constellation*, and Bill Cox also accepted our invitation and spent a full day with us. Both had some helpful suggestions.

The first day Bus sailed *Eagle* against us, we followed the last start of the day with a scrub race back to port. We had our old experimental 2-ply main on and one of our least successful jibs, and *Eagle* walked away from us. We thought nothing of it, realizing how much slower we were with those sails, but all that evening we heard comments from many sources about how *Eagle* had beaten *Constellation* and if only Bus had been her skipper, things would have been different. Needless to say, none of this originated with Bus, a truly fair and self-effacing guy. We felt it unfair to Bill Cox, however, and hence the next day put on our racing sails. We had two scrub races upwind, and in both of them *Constellation* drew ahead, not dramatically but by the same degrees as in the final trials. This confirmed my twin beliefs that Cox had made *Eagle* go fast and that *Constellation* was a slightly faster boat.

It was heart-warming all the unstinting help Bus, Bill and Ted gave us. Those who have never been engaged in competition for the Cup don't share the view of many Americans that it would "be good for the sport" if another country won. Or if they do have that view (and there is something to be said for it), they want to be sure that no stone is left unturned in our preparations for defense. Then if another country were to win it, more power to them, but we must never lose the Cup because of complacency or unwillingness to make an all-out effort in its defense.

Many of our sails were recut in the few days before the match. Nothing drastic was done, but little improvements here and there, and the sails did look just a bit more perfect as a result. I was again impressed, just as I had been before the final trials, by how effective it was to recut existing sails rather than order new ones. Few yachtsmen recut often enough, partly because it's difficult to corral a sailmaker long enough to do the job.

Much of our time during these days while at the dock and even upon returning to Castle Hill was spent talking to television and radio commentators and to reporters for magazines and newspapers. I've never been so photographed in all my life, never been so besieged with questions. Eric went through the same process, as did some of the crew to lesser degree. To her horror, Charlotte kept getting buttonholed for comment on the woman's angle.

It was fun for a while but soon got not only tedious but took time from our preparations. It was hard to break away for the simple reason that almost all of the interviewers were so pleasant, so professional.

The question most asked was how we rated our chances, and I kept saying I thought we would win, simply because I *did* think so. I kept worrying it would come out over the air or through the press that we were cocky, but only once did we read something which so indicated. I've always been impatient with football coaches who have a team loaded with talent (and know it) yet proclaim that their powerhouse will be lucky to win half their games. We did feel we should be favored over *Sovereign,* expected her to be a bit easier to beat than *American*

Eagle, and hence I came right out and said we expected to win. I never said we expected to win in four straight (though in my heart I felt we had a great chance to).

We all felt, and so stated, that *Sovereign* was far from another *Sceptre*, the badly beaten challenger of 1958. She looked like a much better boat, and the fact that she had undergone trials before selection was sure to make her skipper and crew sharper. Hence, when we said we expected a hard-fought match, we were not just being cozy. I believe we were right in assessing *Sovereign* as a marked improvement over *Sceptre*. What we failed to recognize sufficiently was what a truly great boat *Constellation* was.

In the week preceding the match there was one party after another in Newport's grand old mansions. Crews of both *Sovereign* and *Constellation* were invited to all, and urged to attend. We went to several cocktail parties, including a huge blast provided by the Governor of Rhode Island. For the most part, we skipped the dances for the simple reason that our curfew was about the time they started. We did go to a fine dinner dance put on by the British, complete with wild grouse flown over from England. *Kurrewa's* crew stayed till the end, but *Sovereign's* walked out with us just as things were really warming up.

The night before the match, the entire crew had a quiet dinner together at Castle Hill and then turned in early. After all the pressure racing we had gone through against *Eagle*, I climbed the stairs with the belief that sleep would come easily. After all, I couldn't quite believe *Sovereign* would be as tough, so what to worry about? I hadn't reckoned with the fact that it was the America's Cup we were to race for the next day. Sleep came eventually, but only after an hour or more in which I found it impossible to think of anything but start tactics and strategy. I didn't really fear losing if we lost after sailing well, but I couldn't avoid worrying about goofing off, or even fouling out and thus letting down our great boat and great crew which had worked for half a year for this very moment.

On the surface, breakfast the next morning was like any other, but it was eaten faster and all hands took off for the shipyard as soon as it was finished instead of the customary dawdle over a second cup of coffee. The staff of Castle Hill, so used to seeing us go out for a crucial race that they sometimes forgot to wish us luck, were this day bubbling over. Some of them had seen the Australians go forth from these very doors to glorious defeat in *Gretel* just two years before. This time they wanted a winner, and they let us know it.

Even though we arrived at the dock an hour before time to shove off, it was already crowded. Some were friends, some we had never seen, but all wished us well.

The hour went rapidly because we kept busy checking weather reports, deciding on our sail inventory and even getting Bob Blumenstock to measure a spinnaker and a storm jib from *Eagle* which we thought we might use. It all seemed just like any other day. But finally the chores were done, Charlotte kissed me her very best, Rob and Louise, who had played hooky from school for this one day, gave their Dad one of his better farewells and *Chaperone's* engines starting easing us away from the dock. We had been too busy to realize many eyes had been waiting for this moment. Hundreds of boats in the harbor blew their horns in unison. The throng on the dock, with the entire Newport Shipyard gang in the forefront, let go a mighty and impulsive cheer. Suddenly we realized how many people *did* care. The ensign was not on its staff and three of us at once realized that it was vitally important to us that it be there.

A moment later *Sovereign* eased away from *Eagle's* old dock to the accompaniment of almost equal din. As we towed out at 10 knots behind our Coast Guard escort, every boat we passed gave us a big wave. On the shores, cars tooted, men, women and children waved and cheered. One family at Fort Adams unfolded a huge homemade banner reading "Good Luck, Connie." I hope they read this, because it's the only way I have of telling them how good it made us feel.

Some Americans may feel it would be good for the sport for another nation to win the Cup, but rightly or wrongly we got the feeling that those who watched us pass were pulling for us.

As far as the eye could see in all directions there were yachts, steamers, even outboards converging on the America's Cup buoy. Overhead were blimps and planes, and flanking us as we towed toward the scene was a veritable fleet of Navy destroyers, Coast Guard icebreakers and cutters. Sailors are not used to spectators beyond a few friends or families, and to have many thousands out there to see us race made me realize the enormity of the contest we were about to be involved in. We enjoyed the spectacle, enjoyed the excitement it engendered, but at the same time it sobered me. What an audience to watch me hack it up!

⚓ AMERICA'S CUP COURSE ⚓
1964

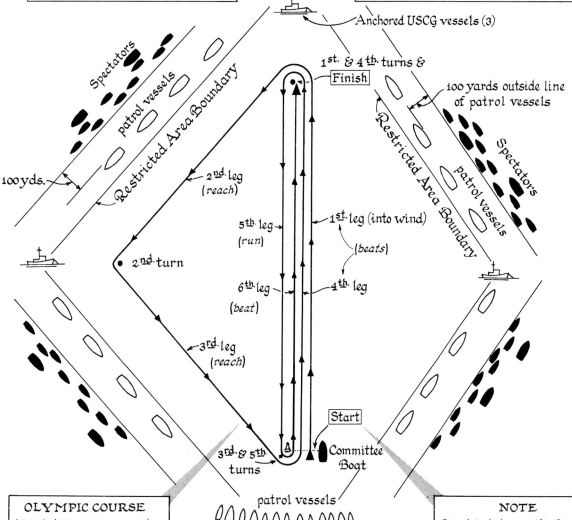

First leg is directly into the wind

wind

Newport

Brenton Reef Light

143° true, 9 miles

Pt. Judith

Start

5 miles radius

Anchored USCG vessels (3)

Spectators

patrol vessels

Restricted Area Boundary

1st. & 4th. turns & Finish

100 yards outside line of patrol vessels

Restricted Area Boundary

Spectators

patrol vessels

100 yds.

2nd. leg (reach)

2nd. turn

5th. leg (run)

1st. leg (into wind)

(beats)

6th. leg (beat)

4th. leg

3rd. leg (reach)

3rd. & 5th. turns

Start

Committee Boat

patrol vessels

OLYMPIC COURSE
Total distance 24.3 miles as the crow flies

NOTE
Start is between the Committee Boat and a special orange & white lighted gong buoy

Spectators

D & H. de F.

Usually I went below on the tow out, but not this day of days. This was a spectacle for anyone, but in particular for the twenty-two of us on *Constellation* and *Sovereign*, who were the focus of all this attention. As usual, we won the towing race out, arrived at the buoy, set our No. 1 main (our winning main), and got our 5-ounce No. 2 on the stay. It was a gorgeous day, appropriate to the occasion and with an 8-knot west-by-south wind which showed signs of building.

After checking the line and finding it square to the wind, Rod, Eric and I had a final discussion of our start strategy. From past experience and from weather broadcasts, we expected the wind to haul clockwise, and this, plus the square line, favored being to windward if possible at the start. It was agreed, however, that it was still more important to insure clear wind at the start, ahead and to windward if possible, but above all else clear. The previous evening Olin Stephens had recommended that our starts be conservative. Obviously he felt confidence in his boat—more, I dare say, than in me. I didn't buy this altogether for the first race. True, I too *thought* we were faster, but I didn't *know*. Also, I felt it would be too comforting to Peter Scott if he detected any apparent timidity on our part. Therefore, while recognizing the logic of Olin's advice, I decided to go after the first start, to be aggressive. I resolved not to press so far as to run the risk of a foul, but with that one reservation planned to go all-out.

The Coast Guard was doing a great job of clearing the vast armada from the race course, and at twelve-fifteen, course signals were hoisted. In just 20 minutes the nineteenth match for the America's Cup would begin. We were reaching back and forth below the line, meeting *Sovereign* on an opposite course every few minutes. We passed each other with 14 minutes to go, and it crossed my mind that Peter Scott just might try to jump us at this early time. Instead, both crews waved gaily to each other and then we went our separate ways.

With 11 minutes to go, we again approached each other, and this time I decided to hook up and try to jump on *Sovereign*'s tail. The crew was so advised but also were told to look casual. You've never seen a more relaxed-looking group as we came bow to bow. Our crew was sprawled about rather than poised at the winches. I tried to look as if I was out for a Sunday afternoon sail, but just as we came abreast put the helm down to swing onto *Sovereign*'s stern. It worked! *Sovereign* bore off after we headed up but not for a few seconds and those seconds of delay put us nicely on her tail, about a length astern.

On the day of the first race the spectator fleet, composed of boats of all sizes and types, stretched as far as the eye could see (top). By the time of the rugged third race, there were still some die hards, but the number had dwindled.

Before the start of the first race on September 15 we got right on "Sovereign's" tail. It gave us the chance to call the shots while she had to worry about being blocked from the starting line.

It was at this moment that Olin Stephens first remarked to Charlotte on *Chaperone*, "I don't like what Bob is doing." But we liked it just fine. Whether we could block *Sovereign* remained to be seen, but with this initial advantage we had removed any risk of being blocked ourselves and could pretty well call our own start.

Peter jibed, tacked, jibed again and tacked again and through it all we followed in his wake, keeping the same distance apart. I was pleased to note we had no difficulty turning as fast as *Sovereign* and in fact felt we could have turned a bit sharper and closed the distance to a point where we might block her from tacking or jibing. I decided not to because that *could* have resulted in a foul if we misjudged anything.

Olin, of course, knew nothing of this bit of restraint and hence, while not disliking our position, was dying a slow death. With five minutes to go, *Sovereign* broke jib and switched from clockwise to counterclockwise circling. We followed suit and maintained our position and distance. This was fun but a deadly serious sort of fun, because one misstep and *Sovereign* could wriggle off the hook and impale us on it instead.

With 2½ minutes to go and while several lengths below the line, *Sovereign* jibed and sharpened up toward the line for still another circle. At this time we decided to part company, to reach instead away from the line, getting enough distance from it to come roaring back with full headway near the weather end. By getting on her tail we had achieved the freedom to do this at our own option and at a time of our choosing, but whether or not we could now also get the start was quite another story. It depended a great deal on timing our run to hit the line at the right instant. It depended even more on what *Sovereign* might do. If she elected to drive off, she could get a well-timed start at the leeward end with good headway. This then would give us the more favorable windward end to ourselves. If she went for the weather end, she could get there only by two tacks, which would reduce her speed, but by so doing, she could have a chance to foul us up if we mistimed our approach.

With 1½ minutes to go, we jibed and came reaching for a spot a length to leeward of the Committee boat. As our speed increased to 9 knots, I could see Peter tack onto port tack with the obvious intent of crossing us and then tacking ahead. If we were late, he could blanket us. If early, we might he unable to kill by bearing off.

With a bit over 30 seconds to go, *Sovereign* tacked dead ahead of us about two lengths distant, just the spot to give us the most difficult choice. We were traveling 2 feet to her one, but if we attempted to pass to windward, I was fearful she might luff up enough before the gun to put us into a barging situation. If we drove off, I suspected our added headways would enable us to drive through her lee and get a good start, albeit not in the spot we wanted.

Things were happening so fast that there was no time for consultation. There never is at the crucial moment of the start. I drove off another point, hollered "Trim for speed," and watched *Sovereign* as we roared for the line at 9½ knots. She could be making no more than 6 knots, and I guessed we could break through. Then I saw her bear off too, to the same reaching course, saw her gaining more headway, but above all else saw that her new course had opened up a wide gap between her and the Committee boat. We were almost overlapped on her leeward quarter as Buddy called, "Two lengths from the line," on the intercom and my watch showed 14 seconds. There was no chance for me to say anything but "Trim," as I said a silent prayer that we could clear *Sovereign*'s stern, and brought *Constellation* up sharply on the wind. Buddy had not called distances because he, like everyone else on *Constellation* and *Sovereign,* had assumed we were going through to leeward. I had thought so too, but the opening to windward and the chance of avoiding her blanket zone were so inviting that a quick switch of plans seemed warranted.

We cleared *Sovereign*'s stern by 20 feet, little enough since we were going a good 2 knots faster at the time. Our great crew trimmed instantly so that we had only a momentary luff. *Sovereign* was caught flat-footed, having assumed when we bore off that we would stay off, and as we crossed the line a few seconds after the gun, we were a length to windward and our bow was 30 feet in front. Rod, as he caught

We are charging for the line at over 9 knots as "Sovereign" tacks on our leeward bow, hoping for a safe leeward position.

We bear off as if to drive through to leeward and surely would have had "Sovereign" held high.

When "Sovereign" wiped off there was no longer any danger of being caught barging so we swung up across her stern, clearing by a few feet and swept to windward.

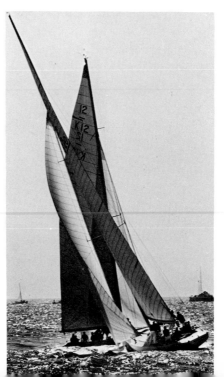

his breath, shouted, "Great start, Bob." Eric put it better—"Best you've made all summer."

I've described it in detail not to try to prove that I'm a hot-shot starter, but rather to show the advantage the tailing position gives and also the risk involved in aggressive tactics. Peter played his role perfectly, but our full headway made it impossible for him to beat us across provided our start was well timed. Had we stayed to leeward, I'm sure we would have broken through and achieved a safe leeward, but going by to windward put us in a still better position. I still shudder a bit, however, about what would have happened had we not been able to clear *Sovereign*'s stern as we swung up. Can't you see the headlines—*Bavier* Rams *Sovereign*, Loses First Race at Start. Both Boats Laid Up for Repairs. But we did clear, and if I race for another 40 years I suspect no moment will retain as fond a spot in my memory as the start of the first race of the nineteenth match for the America's cup.

After the start, *Sovereign* kept her wind clear by driving off, but *Constellation* footed equally as fast and sailed a full point higher.

Within 10 minutes Peter tacked, we tacked on top and, though we didn't know it then, the nineteenth match was as good as over. We led

Seconds before the gun "Constellation" is flying and "Sovereign" driving in hopes of keeping clear air.

Here's how we were as we crossed the line in the first race. Forgive me please for being proud of this start.

We felt a mixture of pride and embarrassment as we waited for "Sovereign" to finish.

On the first reach we held even but "Constellation" has a much larger lead than the camera shows. We were enjoying ourselves immensely.

at the first mark by nearly two minutes, held roughly even on the two reaches, gained a minute on the second windward leg, nearly two minutes on the run and finally won by 5 minutes, 34 seconds. Except on the first leg, there had been little excitement. Thereafter we covered and *Constellation* ate up her opponent.

At the press conference that evening, Peter Scott was asked, among other things, what was the most encouraging thing to him about the first race. His reply, "That we didn't lose by more," was meant to be jocular. Instead, in the light of what happened thereafter, it was prophetic.

The first day the wind did build to 12 knots at times, and there were uncommonly large seas for that amount of wind. The day of the second race, however, forecast a true heavy weather test. It was blowing 17 knots from the south-southwest, with puffs still harder, and big steep seas. Tradition has it that the British like a blow, and by this time

Constellation was known as a great light-weather boat. Here at last was the chance to show whether we could also take a blow—a chance we had been waiting for.

In our conference at Castle Hill following the first race, it was decided we would go after conservative clear wind starts henceforth. I agreed completely because by now we had concrete evidence of our superior speed. At the 10-minute gun for the second race, we passed close to *Sovereign*, but neither boat made any effort to hook up. At 7 minutes, Peter made a halfhearted effort to get on our tail, but did not pursue it when he saw we were not trying to get on his. The thought of close tailing in the heavy winds and even heavier seas appealed to neither of us. With just 2 minutes to go, we made our shot for the leeward end of the line and passed *Sovereign* close aboard as she headed on port tack for the weather end. *Sovereign* later tacked onto starboard and eventually beat us across by 5 seconds as I bore off a bit too far to be sure of not being early. This start was Peter's by that margin, but we had followed our "game plan," had avoided entanglements and had lots of room for *Constellation* to show her stuff. And how she showed it! It took me a minute or two to get her in the groove, a minute in which the two boats sailed even. Then *Constellation* put her head down and went to work. The seas were huge, but instead of climbing over them, we sliced through them, with solid water sweeping our deck till it ran off to leeward before the mast. We were pitching as we partially climbed each sea but were steady compared to *Sovereign*, who was bucking like a bronco and throwing huge sheets of spray.

I've been asked many times why *Constellation* hobbyhorsed so much less. The answer is twofold. First, our weight, both of ballast and equipment, was more concentrated in the middle of the boat, with our ends light. This reduced the pendulum effect as seas were encountered. Probably more important was the above-water shape of the two boats. Our bow was fuller at the waterline and hence not so prone to sink into the trough preceding a sea. Above the waterline we had much less flare and less beam and hence when encountering a sea, our bow was not lifted as much, but instead tended to drive through it. Our stern above water was also finer and hence less prone to lift as the sea worked aft. I also found it vital to keep good speed on. As soon as we dropped below 8 knots, pitching increased. Perhaps *Sovereign*, in trying to point with *Constellation*, lost enough speed to accentuate the pitch-

We went our separate ways in the windy second race. "Constellation" drives for a full headway start to leeward. "Sovereign" heads for a good start to weather, tacking before the starting gun.

← *"Constellation's" amazing pointing superiority is shown here. From our leeward start we eventually worked out to the windward of "Sovereign" and outfooted her at the same time.*

→ *When "Constellation" met a sea she sliced through it. Contrast her steady action to "Sovereign's" (below).*

→ *"Sovereign" had a fine entrance at the waterline but pronounced flare above. This flare lifted her as she met a sea and induced hobby horsing so evident here.*

ing which her basic full form initiated.

But back to the race. Inside of a few minutes *Constellation* not only worked out well ahead, but also pointed so much higher that we were soon dead ahead and then soon thereafter, on *Sovereign*'s weather bow. We could see Peter try pointing with us and drop well astern. Then he would drive off, but even then he footed no faster than we. It was hopeless. Short tacking availed them nothing, either. We seemed to gather way quicker and widened out still more. Our crew work was superb, but we all knew that had we swapped boats, we would have been licked. We like to think we would have made it closer, but in any event, would not have beaten *Constellation*. After 4½ miles of sailing we were a whopping 3 minutes, 43 seconds ahead. We lost 9 seconds on the first reach and another 10 seconds on the third leg, but on the second windward leg, with Eric sailing, picked up 2 minutes. Then on the run, Peter, in desperation, tacked downwind, overdid it, and lost an incredible 7 minutes. I sailed the last leg, gave *Sovereign* a loose cover and saw every tack she made work against her. Just as it became time to tack for the finish, she was lifted and consequently headed on the next tack. We finished at 15:56:48 and it was 16:17:12 before *Sovereign* limped across 20 minutes, 24 seconds later and, mind you, in a good breeze. It was the worst dubbing any Twelve had ever given another, the worst Cup Race defeat of the century.

We were not very happy. Winning is fine, but a slaughter of this magnitude of a friendly foe took the fun out of it. Peter somehow managed a cheerful demeanor at the post-race press conference despite dying inside. It was wisely said that while he never won a race, he also never lost a press conference. For graciousness in defeat Peter Scott has no equal.

Since *Sovereign* signified her unwillingness to start the next day, we had little to do. We saw her out trying out a different main and had the strange experience of hoping it was better. We checked over our gear then took off for a swim at Bailey Beach.

The next day was a carbon copy, weatherwise, of the second race. Peter was more aggressive at the start and got on our tail at a long distance as we tried to avoid entanglements. Then I was late jibing back for the line and Peter jibed inside of me and directly on our wind. I was able to get clear wind by tacking and crossing on port tack. Peter had to wait before tacking to keep from being early, but as we

Peter Scott never lost a press conference. A man accustomed to winning, he was still the most gracious loser I've ever seen. Left to right are "Slim" Sommerville, Peter, Bus Mosbacher, myself and Eric.

crossed was several lengths on our weather beam. He had taken the start and most handsomely.

Then *Constellation* again went to work, ate out ahead, worked up to windward, and despite our deficit at the start, we led by 4 minutes, 7 seconds at the mark. I had never felt *Constellation* so alive, so much in the groove. Our only worry thereafter was a breakdown in the truly mountainous seas and 20-knot wind. But we held together, and while we never quite got back in the groove of that first leg, we did keep widening out to win by 6 minutes, 33 seconds. Peter had sailed a good race, his sails looked better, but he just wasn't a match for us. We were glad to have won, gladder also to have had no 20-minute margin.

That night at the post-mortem we always had, I asked Olin, only half joking, "Shall we try to dazzle them at the start in the next race?" Olin, as I knew he would be, was all for conservative starts and found no fault with the really lousy one I had made that day. But a sailor has pride and I didn't like overhearing an English observer mutter to his friend, "It doesn't matter how lousy a start Bavier gets. That bloody boat bails him out." True enough, but I still didn't like it. It's hard to get a good start while on the defensive, and by this time I felt we had nothing to lose by being aggressive, just so long as we avoided fouls.

I felt even if in the process we were over early, we could still overhaul *Sovereign.*

On Monday, September 21, we had a lovely clear day and an 8–10 knot wind as we jockeyed about the starting area. The seas, built up by three days of strong wind from the east, were enormous. Not so steep as for the third race, but long and lumpy—*Constellation* weather. Peter must have been surprised to have us jump him with 11 minutes to go. We stuck on his tail, despite his best wriggling efforts. Then with 3 minutes to go, he jibed back for the line a bit early—just the right tactic. If we followed him, he could blanket us enough to make us late and still probably kill enough way not to be early himself. If we jibed inside, we would be very early unless we did a lot of killing ourselves. I had no time to ponder the odds, but decided to jibe inside and head back first for the line. Our jib was still not broken out and with those big seas to stop us, I felt we could keep headway down till the last moment.

It worked fine. For the first 30 seconds of our course back we covered only two lengths and by blanketing *Sovereign* made her drop further back. Then with 2 minutes to go, Peter broke his jib out. If we followed suit we would be early, I knew, and hence we let him sail through our lee and into a safe leeward. Our chance now for taking the start lay in breaking jib at precisely the right instant so that we could hit the line on time. If we could do that, *Sovereign* would have to drive off to leeward in order to keep from being early. If she tried to maintain a safe leeward and we timed our start right, she would be over ahead of the gun. Since we had no timed run for the line, it was tough to decide when to break jib, but with a bit more than a minute to go, we snapped it out and *Constellation* started picking up speed. With just 30 seconds to go, Peter still had his safe leeward, still had us in his pocket, but then we saw him running down the line to keep from being over. "Good!" I thought. "We've now got clear air and should wind up with an even start." I was only half right. Peter was determined not to let us get too clear and didn't bear off quite far enough. As the gun sounded, a horn sounded and we saw *Sovereign*'s number displayed. She was over early and by the time she had returned, we were a full minute on top.

That was the end of the boat race, the end of the nineteenth match for the America's Cup. Peter and his crew sailed well, but *Sovereign*

At the third race start I was late coming back. "Sovereign" jibed inside us to this beautiful position. We got clear air by crossing on port tack but this was Peter's start by a big margin. →

simply didn't like the seas. I suspect if the match had been in smooth water the races would have been much closer, though the result the same. Her sails seemed inferior and her rig was certainly crude and heavy when compared to ours. I guess I'm prejudiced, but I also feel our crew did a better job, but as stated earlier, God help us if we had to try to win with *Sovereign.*

In that last race we kept moving out, except on the run when *Sovereign* used a chute they had never raced with before and picked up a full minute. By then it mattered little, as we had been over 13 minutes ahead at the second windward mark. It was an easy race, even dull, since in the moderate winds there was not even the possibility of a breakdown to inject some element of suspense.

Then on the last leg a strange thing happened. We began to notice a growing excitement in this unexciting race. As we tacked in a loose cover, the jib slammed home with the same ferocity as in that crucial race when we broke *American Eagle's* heart. The crew was lined up on the weather rail as usual, minimizing windage, but we saw them talking to each other, glancing back, way back, at *Sovereign.* In the cockpit we kept a steady plot on *Sovereign,* and as she dropped further back and the Committee boat loomed ever larger, I finally realized why we were all getting so excited about a race in which our opponent was still over a mile astern. This was not just a race. This was the culmination of a dream which started nearly twelve months before. This was the last time we who had been sailing together day in and day out for six months would ever be together as a unit. This was the greatest racing sailboat in the world, and we had but one more mile to race before we parted company. This was the conclusion of a match which would extend tradition that had lasted for well over one hundred years. One more tack and we could fetch the line. One more tack and we would be winners of that holy grail to yachtsmen—the America's Cup.

We tacked smartly, saw that our incredibly close-winded thoroughbred was fetching with ease, and I called to our skipper, Eric Ridder, to take her across. He refused. I argued with him, virtually insisting. He still refused. I then urged him to come share the wheel. He again refused. It was my great privilege, therefore, to sail *Constellation* across the line at 16:22:27 Monday, September 21, 1964, to win the America's Cup. It was a proud moment, proudest of my thirty-five years of yacht racing. I've felt many times that it was Eric's finest hour,

"Constellation" can hobby horse too but she keeps moving. This is immediately after the third race start. Our wind is clear and we soon had a commanding lead.

Eric who had worked so hard for so long, who had gathered us all together, had organized us so well, planned so well and now at the precise moment of victory was so completely self-effacing.

As the gun sounded, Rod reached over the leeward gunwale and patted *Constellation*'s topsides and told her she was a good girl. Spontaneously I found myself doing the same. Then we had a mob scene in the cockpit with handshakes, back slapping and war whoops as we all told each other how truly hot stuff we all were. The spectator fleet which had dwindled to a hard core of really keen yachtsmen let out with a din of horn blowing and hand waving. Boats crowded us on both sides, eager to take one last photo of this greyhound of the seas at her moment of final triumph. *Chapérone* eased near, and all I could see was Charlotte looking at me as though we had just become engaged. Could the finish of any other race engender such wild enthusiasm with the second boat nearly two miles astern?

We reached away from the line for 7½ minutes, jibed and reached back and were right on the line and close aboard as *Sovereign* crossed 15 minutes, 40 seconds later than we had.

We cheered each other lustily, an easy chore for us. Then various members of both crews took turns at the wheel as we sailed in company back to Newport. On *Constellation* we all remained on deck, giv-

Note how "Sovereign" throws spray forward as well as aside.
Why is her crew scattered?

"Constellation" throws less spray and all off to the side. When sailing up wind our crew always looked like a neat stack of wood.

ing each other extravagant toasts with champagne which an optimist had put on ice in the bilge. On *Sovereign* most hands went below to do and say we know not what.

As we neared Castle Hill we saw thousands of men, women and children lining the shore, waving frantically. Hundreds of cars tooted in unison. A twenty-one-gun salute came from the frenzied staff at Castle Hill, who saw no need to conserve powder now. Fireboats, their hoses operating full blast, flanked us as we beat into the harbor.

Then we dropped main, *Chaperone* nestled alongside, and eased us into our Newport Shipyard dock where the yard gang and apparently all of Newport had gathered for a noisy welcome.

Shortly, *Sovereign*'s crew came over, we exchanged uniform shirts,

(Below left) On the fourth race start we tailed "Sovereign" and jibed inside her when she went for the line. We were both early. Knowing this, we didn't break jib when "Sovereign" broke hers to clear her wind.

(Below) A minute to go and "Sovereign" has a safe leeward. I still feel she is early but am worried.

(Below left) Now Peter is worried about being early and is giving up his safe leeward. Just twenty seconds to go and we are charging for the line.

(Below right) The gun has gone. "Sovereign's" was early, is going back and we are home free. The race is all over at the start.

dumped each other unceremoniously into the water, and as dusk settled, left *Constellation* to drive back for a joyous celebration at Castle Hill.

Next day in the cold light of dawn we pitched in on the saddening task of stripping *Constellation* of all loose gear and making her ready for the tow back to her builder's yard and a winter layup. Then we went home.

We left behind us not only the greatest racing sailboat in the world, but also memories of 11 months of planning, 6 months of continuous sailing with a great bunch of guys, early disappointments, an exciting comeback and eventual triumph tinged with anticlimax. Had the great effort been worthwhile? Are you kidding?

As we cross the line to win the Cup for America, Rod and I give "Constellation" the pat she so richly deserves.

←

"Sovereign's" great reaching chute gained her a full minute on this leg. It was used only once. The lead over the main leach is right. It spoils the main a bit but frees the spinnaker leach for greater efficiency.

We toast each other and "Constellation" with champagne while waiting for "Sovereign" to finish.

Fireboats escort "Sovereign" and "Constellation" as they near their docks for the last time. Suddenly six months of sailing didn't seem so long. ↓

*"Sovereign's" crew comes aboard to
congratulate us. It was easy for us to
smile as the crews swapped uniform
shirts.*

*Buddy Bombard swaps shirts with
Valerie Boyden to the amusement of
Tony Boyden and Phillip Scott, who
needed something to smile about
after their crushing defeat.* ➡

Peter and his "Sovereign" gang wave goodbye bedecked in our uniforms. We saw them once again at our victory party that night. No crew was ever more gracious in defeat.

Goodbye to "Constellation", the greatest sailboat I have ever sailed or doubtless ever will sail, the boat which made a dream come true. →